Kidarwalks

IN
LANCASHIRE

Ron Freethy

COUNTRYSIDE BO
NEWBURY BERKSHI

First published 2009
© Ron Freethy 2009

COUNTRYSIDE BOOKS
3 Catherine Road
Newbury, Berkshire

To view our complete range of books,
please visit us at
www.countrysidebooks.co.uk

ISBN 978 1 84674 141 8

Photographs by the author
Maps by Pam Pheasant

Produced through MRM Associates Ltd., Reading
Typeset by Mac Style, Beverley, East Yorkshire
Printed by Information Press, Oxford

Contents

AREA MAP SHOWING LOCATION OF THE WALKS

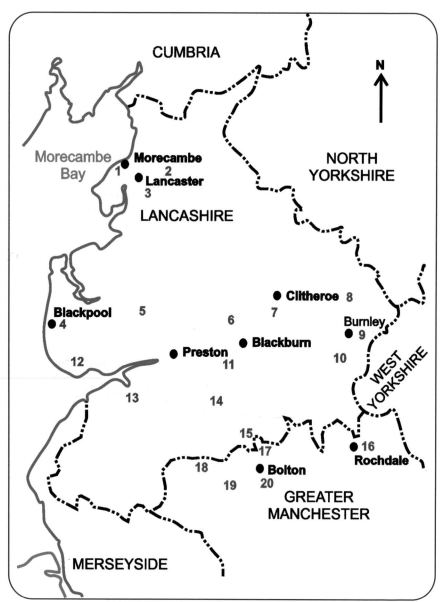

Contents

PUBLISHER'S NOTE

We hope that you obtain considerable enjoyment from this book; great care has been taken in its preparation. Although at the time of publication all routes followed public rights of way or permitted paths, diversion orders can be made and permissions withdrawn.

We cannot, of course, be held responsible for such diversion orders and any inaccuracies in the text which result from these or any other changes to the routes nor any damage which might result from walkers trespassing on private property. We are anxious though that all details covering the walks are kept up to date and would therefore welcome information from readers which would be relevant to future editions.

The simple sketch maps that accompany the walks in this book are based on notes made by the author whilst checking out the routes on the ground. They are designed to show you how to reach the start, to point out the main features of the overall circuit and they contain a progression of numbers that relate to the paragraphs of the text.

However, for the benefit of a proper map, we do recommend that you purchase the relevant Ordnance Survey sheet covering your walk. The Ordnance Survey maps are widely available, especially through booksellers and local newsagents.

Introduction

This book is aimed at those looking for somewhere to take active children so they can get plenty of exercise in the open air whilst ensuring that there is something to interest the grown ups too.

It is not just young mums who look after children these days. Fathers also play their part and, in the case of single parents or where both partners have to work, the grandparents – much more active in retirement than in times gone by – also do their bit. During one of my walks I came across an 80-year-old great-grandma who was teaching some children the old song, 'The good ships came down the alley-alley oh, the alley-alley oh', – a reminder of the days of the canals when barges did sail through narrow alleys of water.

Lancashire is lucky in that many former sites of heavy industry have been converted into beautiful country parks. I met a grandfather, his daughter and her toddlers at Pennington Flash near Leigh. He was telling the children about his work in the coal mine that was once on the site – one of the largest in the world. At Moses Gate near Bolton I watched a grandma sketching the birds on the water and telling the youngsters about working in the mill where paper was made. The children were spellbound as they listened to her.

Lancashire's industrial sites have always been surrounded by glorious unspoiled countryside and close to ancient houses and the estates associated with them. These provide a real contrast to the industrial landscape. I hope that this book will give children a balanced perspective, provide them with the opportunity for strenuous exercise and encourage an interest in their surroundings. Just as important has been the need to ensure that those looking after these agile young people have quiet places from which to watch their charges whilst enjoying the history and beauty of the places they visit.

If there are tired and happy children at the end of each of these strolls, then this book will have been well worth writing.

Ron Freethy

1

The Stone Jetty

Hopscotch on the Jetty

The Stone Jetty.

There is activity all the way for children on this walk through some spectacular scenery, plus lots of railway and pleasure steamer history to be enjoyed. The children's games laid out along the old jetty are interspersed with rest areas with benches and fascinating stone statues. This is a place where the balance between allowing youngsters freedom and keeping a watchful eye open for their safety is easily achieved.

Kiddiwalks in Lancashire

Getting there *From the M6 turn off at Junction 34 and follow the signs for Morecambe. Follow the signs to the Promenade passing the station. There are numerous car parks, some of which are pay and display.*

Length of walk 1½ miles
Time 2 hours
Terrain Very easy, with paved areas mostly on the level and very suitable for pushchairs. Except for crossing the A589, there is no traffic and youngsters can run about to their hearts' content.

The Walk

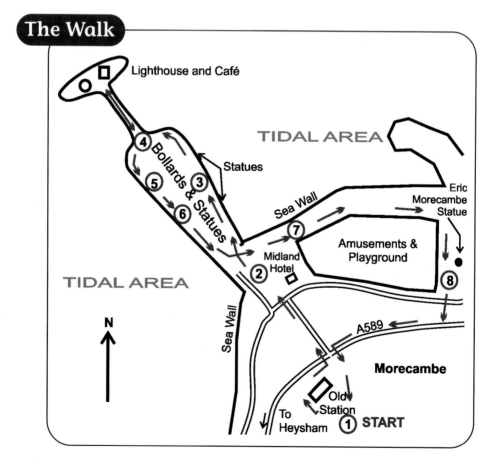

The Stone Jetty

Start/Parking The walk starts at the Morecambe Visitor Information Centre (GR 428644).
Map OS Explorer 296, Lancaster, Morecambe & Fleetwood
Refreshments There is a wide choice of cafés and food outlets all around Morecambe. Until 2008 the Midland Hotel was all but derelict but following a multi-million pound investment it is now open to the public and families are welcome. There is an outdoor patio area overlooking the Stone Jetty and there is an affordable child-friendly menu. The Midland was built in the 1930s by the then very rich Midland Railway Company and was famous for its decor. It is now a fine reminder of the gracious living of that period.

There is also a café with tables in and around the railway building on the Stone Jetty.

1 The old Midland Railway station complex is now an Information Centre and well worth an extended visit. From here turn right for a short distance along the A589 and then cross the road and turn left. After a short distance turn right onto the wide promenade and then turn right again.

2 Approach the Midland Hotel which has a large conservatory area which fits in perfectly with

◆ Fun Things to See and Do ◆

The Stone Jetty is a cross between an adventure playground and a birdwatching site. Youngsters meet new friends and some of the **games** are delightfully competitive. Some of these colourful games can be strenuous and are designed to get those little legs moving fast.

There are bird **sculptures** set on raised plinths and others incorporated into the wrought-iron safety barriers. Fun can be had by counting the sculptures on one side of the stone pier and comparing these with those on the opposite side.

Youngsters love identifying the species in the sculptures and looking out into the bay to search for the same birds in the flesh.

Kiddiwalks in Lancashire

1

the rules governing its status as a listed building. Another feature is the family-friendly outdoor patio overlooking the sea. Turn onto the Stone Jetty keeping the bollards to the left.

❸ Stop at the bird maze. Youngsters have great fun following the complex route. Each part of the maze has a bird theme and all around the jetty area are bird sculptures of the species that occur around Morecambe Bay. Continue following the sculpture trail and pass the anglers in search of a good catch.

❹ The café and lighthouse associated with the steamer pier has tables outside that have been given plenty of space so that pushchairs and wheelchairs can be accommodated. There is also a waiter service which means young children with only one adult in attendance can be served in safety. Continue following the statue trail towards the Promenade, still keeping the bollards to your left.

❺ Approach the magpie hopscotch game. This is the traditional game, but with a bird theme and a bird statue overlooks the game. To the numbers are

On the promenade.

added a rhyme associated with magpies:

One for sorrow
Two for mirth
Three for a wedding
Four for a birth
Five for the rich
Six for a witch …

There are egg-shaped stones on which young competitors can have a rest. Continue along the jetty.

❻ After the magpie hopscotch comes the bird word puzzle area. This has a jumble of letters spread out over a wide area. The children can follow the letters on foot and pick out the names of the birds which can be seen around the bay. Continue along the jetty to reach the promenade.

The Stone Jetty

7 Turn left along the promenade to reach the amusement area on the right. For the young and active with energy remaining, this is the perfect area. Continue along the promenade to reach the statue of Eric Morecambe. The comedian was a keen birdwatcher.

8 Turn right at the statue and then right onto the pavement of the A589. After a short distance turn left to the old station where the walk started.

Background Notes ◆

Morecambe is a seaside resort which has at last started to market its greatest asset, the wonderful bay with a backdrop of the Lake District mountains. It has done this without compromising the more traditional attractions such as arcades, fast food outlets and other attractions so beloved by children.

From the 1850s Morecambe Promenade Station was one of the busiest in the north-west and trains brought visitors from the mill towns of Lancashire and Yorkshire. The main station these days is much smaller and closer to the centre of town. Fortunately the grand old station building which was built in 1907 has now been converted into an arts centre. An even older reminder of the steam railway age is a building dating to between 1853 and 1867 which still stands on the recently-renovated Stone Jetty. This was the terminus of a short branch line linking the Promenade station with the steamer pier which was very busy until the 1940s.

At one time the Stone Jetty area was also the base for Ward's ship-breaking enterprise. Liners were scrapped here until the 1930s and during the First World War captured German U-boats were broken up on this site. After a period of dereliction the Stone Jetty has now become part of the Tern Project, a programme designed to display unique artworks along the promenade in Morecambe.

Crook of Lune

On the Tracks

On the edge of the woodland.

A disused railway line, two historic bridges, a sweeping curve of a river and a pretty stretch of woodland make this a walk to remember. The views here are so magnificent that famous painters have been attracted to the scene. The mix of bird song and trickling water is irresistible, as are the sights of colourful birds and a variety of flowers and fungi.

Getting there *From Lancaster follow the A683 towards Kirkby Lonsdale. Just before Caton, a left turn signed Halton leads across the twisting loop of the river and the old railway line. The car park is on the right just after the road has ascended and twisted between high hedgerows.*

The Walk

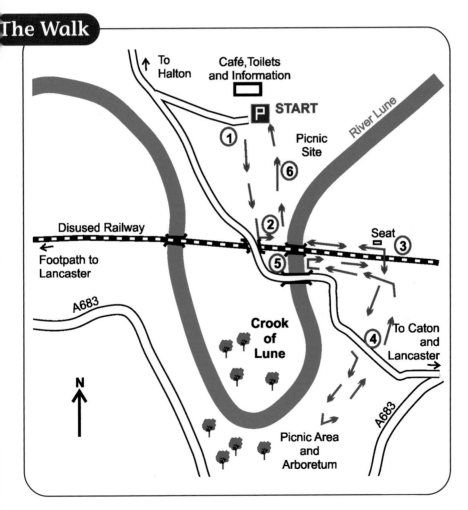

Kiddiwalks in Lancashire

2

Length of walk 1½ miles
Time 2 hours
Terrain For pushchairs there is one set of steps to negotiate but most of the going is easy. These steps can be avoided by using the sloping ramp from the picnic site to the old railway track.
Start/Parking At the car park (GR 522646)
Map OS OL41, Forest of Bowland & Ribblesdale
Refreshments At the car park there are toilets, information and a splendid little café which has substantial snacks, with a menu that is very child-friendly. It is open daily except Monday and Tuesday (other than Bank Holidays).

There are plenty of hostelries in and around the village of Halton including the White Lion and the Ship Inn. To the east of Caton, in Brookhouse, is the Black Bull, where on the nearby bridge is a plague stone – a hollow stone where plague sufferers placed money (in vinegar to kill off any germs). Traders collected the money and left food in exchange. There is no plague in this day and age, only good food on offer for hungry families.

1 From the car park and café follow the signs for the Millennium Walk and descend six wooden steps to reach the track of the old railway. Turn left.

◆ Fun Things to See and Do ◆

On the walk at point 2 there are several **sycamore trees** and in autumn youngsters can have a wonderful time with the seeds, which are shaped like the rotor blades of a helicopter and spin in the breeze. Great fun can be had by seeing how far the seeds fly when they are tossed up into the wind.

If you visit St Wilfrid's church in Halton you will find the **ancient cross** that is said to have been carved by Norsemen over 1,000 years ago. If you have some paper and pencils with you, youngsters will enjoy drawing the symbols that they find on each side of the stone. Examine the walls of the church and look for the Roman altars incorporated in the walls.

2 Cross the old railway bridge. To the left is the sweep of the River Lune and to the right is the substantial road bridge and the wall leading up to it. Approach a wooden seat on the left.

3 At the seat turn right to reach a wooden gate and a sign indicating riverside walk. Descend a field with the river down to the right. Approach another gate.

The River Lune.

4 Pass through the gate and carefully cross the country road. Turn left and then almost immediately right through a metal gate to the Memorial Forest. This is being regularly added to by families wishing to remember a loved one by planting a tree. Here is another delightful picnic spot and an area where youngsters can feed the numerous and ever-hungry ducks. In dry weather the memorial woodland is very child-friendly and is a wonderful place to enjoy a strenuous game of hide-and-seek or other energy-burning activities.

From the picnic site retrace your steps to the start of Point 4. Ascend the track through the field and just before Point 3 look to the left to see a footpath leading down to the river. Descend towards the Lune.

5 Approach a wooden footbridge over a stream leading to the river. Cross the bridge and find a set of steps leading down to the main river. Here is a safe, shallow stretch which is a great place to enjoy a session of Pooh sticks. Then continue along the path. Spend some time under the huge arches of the railway bridge looking for the marks made by the workmen's tools as they shaped the stones to fit into the bridge. Retrace your steps to Point 3. Turn left at the seat and approach Point 2. Instead of ascending the steps to the car park, bear right and walk up the track to a substantial picnic site.

6 From here there are magnificent views over the Lune. This view was painted by J M W

◆◇◆◇◆◇◆◇◆◇◆◇◆◇◆◇◆◇◆◇◆

Turner (1775–1851) before the railway and road bridges were built. He later returned and painted the railway bridge. A few years ago I watched a school party of seven-year-olds drawing this same view and what a splendid job they made of it. Turn left from the picnic site and return to the car park.

◆ Background Notes ◆

In 1849 a railway line was built from Lancaster Green Ayre station along the valley of the River Lune up to the lovely village of Wennington. It was constructed by the **North Western Railway Company** and was soon known as the Little North Western to distinguish it from the much more important London North Western Railway. The Lunesdale company was never very efficient and was always short of rolling stock. They even bought some stock which was too wide, too low and too heavy. The width of the doors in particular meant that if they were opened on entry to the station waiting passengers were in danger of being swept away.

In 1852 the Midland Railway took over and ran the line more efficiently. In 1923 the Lune line was taken over by the LMS (London, Midland and Scottish Railway) until 1947 when the railway system was nationalised. Cutbacks meant that the line was closed to passengers in 1966 and soon after also to goods trains. The lines have gone and the track is now a linear footpath and part of this delightful stroll.

Nearby at **Halton** is a fascinating slice of even older history. Overlooking the church is a hill on which once stood an ancient wooden castle. This was one of the homes of Earl Tostig who was the brother of King Harold, killed at the Battle of Hastings. William of Normandy took over the Saxon lands and his followers decided that their power base would be at Lancaster where they built a huge castle. They thought that Halton Castle could be a focus for a Saxon rebellion.

Williamson Park

A Flutter among the Butterflies

Inside the butterfly house.

This is a stroll through woodlands with many huge trees, some of which have identification labels. The views from the Ashton memorial are spectacular and the terraced paths and undulating terrain almost hide the fact that there was once a huge quarry here which provided stone for some of Lancaster's wonderful old buildings. Look at some of the exposed rock faces and think that all this stone had to be quarried and shaped, not by machines, but by hand. There are lots of nooks and crannies ideal for playing hide-and-seek.

Kiddiwalks in Lancashire

3

Getting there *Williamson Park is only a few minutes' drive from either Junction 33 or 34 of the M6 motorway and it is also signed from the A6. Turn off Wyresdale Road to the car park.*

Length of Walk 1½ miles
Time 2 hours
Terrain Very easy with gentle, well maintained inclines. There

are plenty of seats strategically placed to provide spectacular views.

Start/Parking The moderately-priced pay and display car park off Wyresdale Road. It is open throughout the year, except Christmas Day, Boxing Day and New Year's Day. There are toilets. (GR 492615)

Map OS Explorer OL41, Forest of Bowland & Ribblesdale

The Walk

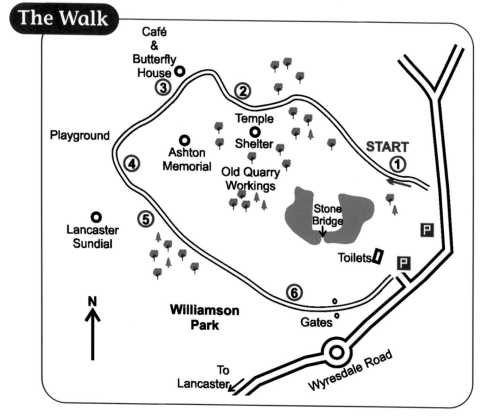

Refreshments Hot and cold meals are available at the Pavilion Café and Shop (telephone 01524 33318). The menu is varied and prices are reasonable. Snacks and drinks are also on offer. The history of the café building itself is fascinating. It was brought to Lancaster in the 1990s from a Garden Festival held in Stoke-on-Trent.

1 From the car park follow the signs to the Ashton Memorial. The wide path ascends steeply through trees with outcrops of rock, a reminder of the days when this was a huge quarry. During the American Civil War in the 1860s supplies of raw cotton were cut off and there was major unemployment. To provide work, paths were laid out with views across the hills overlooking Lancaster.

◆ Fun Things to See and Do ◆

 A visit to the **butterfly house** will delight young and old alike and so will the mini-beast section where the life of invertebrates is explained. There are always members of staff on duty to explain the life of insects and details of a tropical rainforest. Look carefully at the vegetation and you will find eggs, caterpillars and pupae, as well as adult butterflies.

In the butterfly house youngsters will enjoy climbing the spiral staircase leading from the lower level of the rainforest to the canopy. There are seats from which to watch the butterflies, some of which will actually land on visitors if they keep still.

Near the butterfly house and café there are child-friendly **telescopes** from which there are views over Morecambe Bay.

The **adventure playground** is one of the best around. Families can also enjoy a barbecue in an area especially laid out for them. There are open spaces where games can be enjoyed and the viewing platform on the Ashton memorial should not be missed.

The fountain near the end of the walk

2 Suddenly the memorial comes into view. It always creates a gasp of surprise because it seems so large, standing as it does, on a rise. Approach the memorial on the left.

3 A right turn leads to the café and the tropical butterfly house. There are exotic species on the wing throughout the year. Like our native peacock butterfly, many species have coloured rings on their wings which resemble eyes. As the wings open and close these eyes 'flash' and scare away predators. There are also collections of small birds and mini beasts, whilst the colourful gardens attract native butterflies during the warmer months. From the butterfly house return to the viewing area and then descend the obvious path. Enjoy the views of Morecambe Bay and the River Lune straight ahead. Here is the large and very impressive adventure playground.

4 The path twists and turns before reaching an amphitheatre on the left. This provides a sitting place where children can watch wildlife, make notes and sketch. There are lots of grassy areas to play on.

5 The path ascends gently towards a fascinating sundial seen to the right. This was designed in the year 2000 by Ripley St Thomas School and is on the site of the old bandstand long since demolished. The sundial is in the form of a clock with each hour sponsored by a Lancaster company. Continue to follow the winding path, taking the time to study native trees, especially the splendid oaks.

6 Follow the path around keeping the pond on the left. The lake has been refurbished and the footpath passes a waterfall, a fountain and a solid stone bridge. There are sheltered spots ideal for picnics. An obvious path winds left at the pond, passes through an arch, then turns left to return to the car park along a path parallel to the road.

Background Notes ◆

Many people drive along the M6 motorway and see the **Ashton memorial** above the road without realising that it can be visited. The Ashton memorial was saved from the brink of destruction in the late 1980s. It stands overlooking the 54 colourful acres of Williamson Park given to the citizens of Lancaster by the father of James Williamson. James was born in Church Street in 1842, by which time his father had built up a successful business manufacturing oil cloth. James proved to be even more astute and when he died in 1930 he had amassed a fortune of £9.5 million – what he would have been worth today we can only make a guess at, but it would take your breath away! James gave lots of money to improve his native city and he was the major employer in the area for around half a century. He was a forceful Member of Parliament and he deserved to be created Lord Ashton. He developed the park between 1877 and 1882 and he was determined to construct a memorial to celebrate the life of his wife and family. It rises to 220 ft over the Lune valley. A viewing gallery runs around it and the city of Lancaster is laid out below. Beyond the city can be seen the river with the old ports of Sunderland Point on one bank and Glasson Dock on the other. Both these ports are worth a visit and have walks around them that are also suitable for families.

The footpaths running around the site have been landscaped and can be used by wheelchairs and pushchairs. Even the gradients have been carefully designed to assist these wheeled vehicles. The whole park is dog friendly so the family pet need not be left out.

There is a small fee to enter the tropical butterfly house and also to reach the viewing platform.

Stanley Park

Jumbo Jetland

Fountains, statues and colourful flower beds adorn the park.

The whole of Blackpool revolves around fun for people of all ages, with the Pleasure Beach, three piers and exciting entertainment. Those in search of plenty to do but wanting a safe area to explore should not miss Stanley Park. On one side of the park is the zoo and on the other a model village. The circular walk around the park is the perfect place to allow eager youngsters to explore without having to be watched closely because of traffic and crowds along the pavements.

Open-top buses run around Blackpool and journeys can be broken at various stops including the model village, the zoo and, of course, Stanley Park. This is a 'hop-on-hop-off' journey which should not be missed and is particularly enjoyable at illumination time in the autumn.

Getting there *From the M55 motorway turn off at Junction 4 and follow the signs for Victoria Hospital. Along the A587 road there is limited free parking but there is an extensive pay and display car park at the zoo. The model village also has car parking for patrons.*

Length of walk 1½ miles
Time 2 hours
Terrain Very easy with few undulations and one set of easily-negotiated stone steps.

Start/Parking At the entrance to the park (GR 329360).
Map OS Explorer 286, Blackpool & Preston
Refreshments There is a large restaurant in the park and a small snack bar by the side of the boating lake.

① From the roadside car park keep the metal railings and the lake on the right. Just before the model village there is a sign for the De Vere hotel.

◆ Fun Things to See and Do ◆

Around Stanley Park are plenty of **playgrounds** and the **boating lake** is very popular. There are also putting greens and crazy golf courses plus other amenities to exercise young limbs, including a nature trail, lots of steps to climb around the bandstand area and in and around the gardens and fountains. **Motor-boats** can be hired and a little **road train** takes trips around the park.

Look at the **statues** around the lakeside terrace, gardens and fountains. Some statues are of people with bare feet and one has only four toes. Youngsters can have fun finding out which one has the toe missing. There are also statues of lions. How many statues are there? How many show people, how many show animals and how many are in water?

The Walk

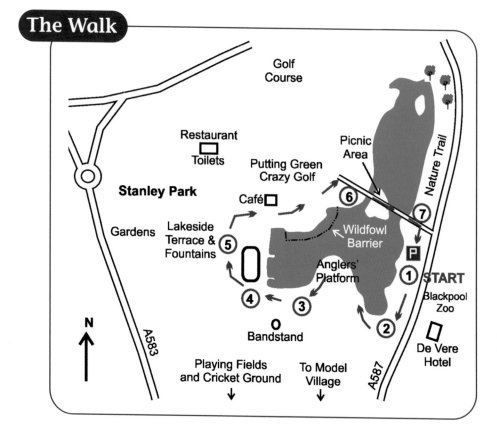

2 Almost opposite the De Vere hotel sign turn right into the park. The lake is soon reached and is very popular with anglers. The views of the lake out to the right reveal wildfowl and small motorboats chugging along together.

3 Approach the magnificently restored bandstand on the left.

The magnificent restored

Footpaths from this area lead to football and cricket fields and to the model village. The substantial path sweeps to the right.

4 At the boat jetty take time to watch the colourful little road train. Turn away from the lake and bear left to a set of stone steps.

5 At the top of the steps is the Lakeside terrace, fountains, statues and gardens. This is a really exciting splash of water and colour and there are plenty of seats from which to enjoy views of the gardens. From the terrace turn right and pass an area of fencing on the right. Then sweep right and descend the gentle incline to the café. Bear left and keep the lake on the right. Look for the wildfowl barrier which is kept free from boats and anglers and allows the birds a sanctuary.

6 Approach two substantial white bridges over the boating lake. Turn right and pass over the first of these bridges. There is a picnic site to the left. Then cross the second bridge. Head towards the park exit.

7 Before leaving the park, look out to the left to see the entrance to the Nature Trail running alongside the lake. For those with the energy to spare taking this trail would add another half mile to the walk but leisure time should be allowed to stop, stare and perhaps feed the birds. Continue to the A587 and turn right to the roadside car park.

◆ Background Notes ◆

Stanley Park was constructed in 1926, partly to provide labour for the unemployed. In 2007 a lottery-funded restoration costing more than £5 million has meant that the park is now in magnificent condition.

The site of the zoo was Blackpool's airport at one time and visitors can still see the old clubhouse which is now the zoo offices. They can also see the old aeroplane hangars that are home to the elephants. This gives a whole new meaning to 'Jumbo' jets.

5

Beacon Fell

A Good and Ugly Stroll

What an ugly face!

This is a wild and wonderful place with several paths laid out through conifer woodland. There are squirrels and birds, including owls and woodpecker, and plenty of tall trees around, where children can play in safety. This is truly a family day out – marvellous views, wildlife, games and parking all free – what a bargain!

Getting there *From the A6 between Preston and Garstang a brown sign indicates Beacon Fell. Follow these signs. The fell is also signed from the attractive village of Chipping. The signs lead to a one-way system running around the fell to the substantial free car park.*

Length of walk 1½ miles
Time 2 hours
Terrain The paths can be used with pushchairs but after rain they can be muddy and wellingtons would be needed. The undulating route involves gradients and one set of easily negotiated wooden steps.

The Walk

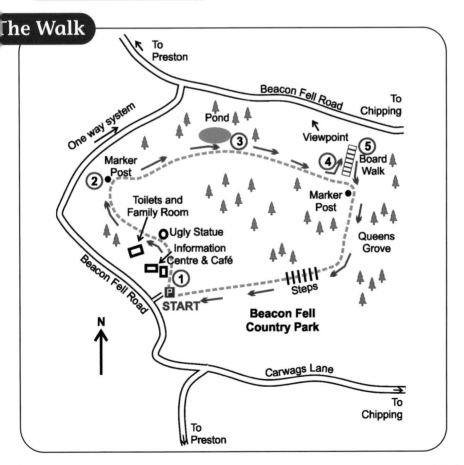

Kiddiwalks in Lancashire

5

Start/Parking At the car park of Beacon Fell (GR 565427).
Map OS Explorer OL41, Forest of Bowland and Ribblesdale
Refreshments There is an excellent café at the Information Centre at Beacon Fell. Snacks and substantial meals are available and there is an extensive outdoor eating area, as well as a clean and modern indoor area for use on the cooler days or even to provide shade in hot weather. Families are well catered for. The visitor centre is open daily. Signed from the fell is the Carwags barbecue area for those who want to cook their own food. There are plenty of pubs and cafés in Chipping.

1 Pass to the right of the café and ascend a cobbled path to reach a carved stone head on the right. Throughout the woodland area there are a number of statues – weird shapes and mythical animals. There is a stone carving showing an ugly face and lots of fun can be had by seeing who can make the most grotesque faces. From here bear left and the wide track changes from cobbles to flattened earth.

2 Approach a post on the left. Do not go straight ahead here but turn sharp right and climb sharply up into the conifers. Here is a hide-and-seek area for children and there are lots of

◆ Fun Things to See and Do ◆

In recent years the fell has been planted up with **trees**, mostly conifers. Among the species are spruce, pine and larch. There is a simple way of distinguishing these. All you have to do is to pull off a leaf. Spruce leaves come off singly; pine leaves break off in pairs whilst the larch leaves come off in lumps. Thus we have S for spruce and single, P for pine and pairs and L for larch and lump! Larch is also the only conifer in Britain which sheds its leaves in the autumn.

In the village of Chipping about three miles to the east is the **Bowland Wild Boar park** set in 65 acres (telephone 01995 61554). Apart from a variety of animals there are swings, slides, pedal vehicles, a tractor ride and a café.

cones on the ground. Some, but not all, have been partly eaten by grey squirrels. The intact cones can be collected and decorated and make excellent free Christmas displays.

3 Approach the pond on the left. In the summer this can be covered in green duckweed but in the spring it is worth looking out for frogs, toads and newts. Bear right at the pond onto a path which can be muddy after rain. There is an alternative and dry route which winds its way in and out of the trees. Approach another marker post.

4 Turn left at the marker post and along a boardwalk to the viewpoint at the summit of the fell.

5 From the viewpoint return to the marker post and go straight ahead. There is now a steep descent through an avenue of trees called Queens Grove. Go down a set of wide and easy-to-negotiate wooden steps and the car park and café can be seen through the trees. Return to the starting point.

◆ Background Notes ◆

Although **Beacon Fell** is only 873 ft above sea level its summit dominates the west Lancashire plain, with Blackpool Tower clearly visible on a good day, whilst to the east the Bowland hills are laid out in all their splendour.

No wonder the summit has been used as one of a chain of beacon hills since the Bronze Age. By lighting fires on the summits vital signals could be transmitted with surprising speed – providing of course that it was not foggy! Beacon Fell was certainly made ready in 1588 when the Spanish Armada approached England, and also between 1795 and 1815 when Britain was threatened by Napoleon's French forces.

During the Second World War, Fell House Farm stood on the site now occupied by the visitor centre. German aircrews had this farm on their maps and used it as a navigation point on their way to bomb Liverpool and Manchester.

6

Ribchester

A Roman Ramble

The Roman Museum sits next to St Wilfrid's church.

Here is an opportunity for youngsters to sit in a Roman bath, and expend lots of energy in the adventure playground which was once the Roman parade square. Add to this a riverside stroll, one of the most family-friendly museums devoted to life in Roman Lancashire and a wide choice of places to eat and you have a perfect outing. You don't always need the sun to shine but, as always, it helps!

Getting there *Ribchester is signed off the A59 road linking Preston with Blackburn and Clitheroe. Follow the signs to Ribchester and cross a bridge over the River Ribble. Follow the pay and display car park signs.*

Length of walk 1½ miles
Time 2 hours
Terrain On the flat and mostly suitable for pushchairs. Following very wet weather there is one muddy section close to the Roman bathhouse but this is never impassable.

The Walk

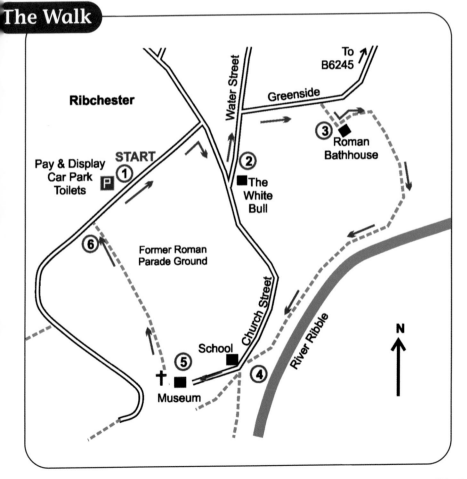

Kiddiwalks in Lancashire

Start/Parking The village car park is pay and display and there are toilet facilities (GR 649354).
Map OS Explorer 287, West Pennine Moors
Refreshments There are good pubs in the village which welcome children and there are also teashops and places to buy ice cream. All around the walk there are seats and picnic tables ideal for those who prefer to bring their own food.

1 From the car park turn left and stop for a while in the sculpture garden on the right. This has a Roman theme and despite the modern figures the display looks to be pure Roman. From the garden turn right and follow the main street.

2 Turn left along Water Street and look out for a row of cottages. These were once part of a coaching inn called the Red Lion. At the cottages on Greenside turn right along a narrow road.

3 Take the first right to approach the Roman bathhouse. It is worth spending time looking closely and reading the labels on each section. This is open free of charge from Easter to the end of October. Here are cold rooms, hot rooms, a plunge bath and also

shown clearly is the underfloor heating system called a hypocaust.

From the bathhouse turn right and follow the path towards the River Ribble. Here is the one very short section that can be difficult, but not impossible, for wheelchairs. Look out for heron and kingfisher. Also find an indicator board showing the levels of the river at various times of drought or flood.

4 At the school, on the right, leave the riverside path and turn left along the narrow road. Keep the river on the left and old cottages with Roman stones incorporated in them to the right.

5 At the vicarage turn sharp right to reach the Roman Museum. Do not miss this chance to walk into Roman history. There are plenty of Roman artefacts including leather shoes, jewellery and even children's toys. There are postcards and booklets for sale.

From the museum enter the churchyard and look out for a late 17th-century sundial with an inscription which reads: *I am a shadow. So art thou. I mark time. Dost thou?*

6 Time should be marked and not wasted in and around St

Wilfrid's church which has a hagioscope. Also known as a leper's squint, this is a hole in the wall through which those who had diseases could watch the service inside without infecting the healthy people. Try finding the hagioscope and squinting through it. Inside there is a 14th-century wall painting of St Christopher, the patron saint of travellers. This dates to the time when travellers had to cross a deep ford over the Ribble before the present road bridge was built.

From the churchyard turn right through a metal gate and along the ramparts of the fort. Here it can be seen that over the centuries the Ribble has changed its course. As this happened large areas of the fort were submerged and have been lost. Continue along the obvious grassy rampart path and through a wooden stile. Turn right onto a metalled road leading back to the car park, with the Roman parade ground, now a children's play area, on the right.

◆ Fun Things to See and Do ◆

At the **Roman Museum** find out how much food was needed to supply one man and his horse. Then multiply this by 500 and go from there to look at the huge granaries.

List the other people who would be needed to keep the **soldiers** functioning efficiently. There would be cooks, blacksmiths, shoemakers, bakers and many others. The soldiers often had their wives and children with them, too.

Spend time at the **Roman bathhouse** and compare this to the bathroom at home. Children love sitting in the old plunge bath and imagining this full of cold water. Look around the village and the church and identify Roman stones.

Visit the **playground** where games can be played whilst thinking about the Roman parade ground below. The Romans trained by marching 1000 paces as fast as they could. Why not try to copy them – try one hundred paces first.

◆ Background Notes ◆

Ribchester has been settled since the Bronze Age and here was one of the largest Roman forts to be found anywhere in Britain. Ribchester is actually the only village set directly on the bank of the River Ribble.

The fort was constructed in AD 79 and helped to subdue the Celtic tribe called the Brigantes. The Roman name was then Bremetannacum Veteranorum and it was placed on the Ribble to protect the roads from Manchester, Carlisle, York and the Roman wall. As many as 500 cavalry were stationed at the fort and excavations have revealed a parade ground on the site of the present children's adventure playground, as well as granaries and the remains of once impressive ramparts. There is an excellent museum built in 1914 that is open throughout the year from 11am to 5pm and has special displays set out for young people. There is a small entry fee.

St Wilfrid's church is one of the finest Norman buildings in Lancashire and is almost always open. There are guides on sale, some written for children. One excellent guidebook points out where stones from the Roman fort have been 'stolen'. All through the village, buildings have incorporated Roman stones; the porch of the White Bull pub is supported by massive Roman pillars and some cottages have Roman altars in their walls.

About a mile outside the village is the hamlet of **Stydd** where the almshouses, built in 1726, were constructed of material from Ribchester Roman fort, including more pillars and an impressive outside staircase. Also at Stydd is a fascinating chapel built by the Knights Hospitalers in the 12th century. The knights went on the Crusades, not just to fight, but also to heal. The modern word 'hospital' derives from these knights. They had a herb garden attached to the chapel and it is worth looking for some of the plants which still grow there.

Spring Wood

A Hop, Skip and a Spring into the Woods

A picnic opportunity near the start of the walk.

Whalley means 'a place of wells' and the Cistercian monks who came here in the 14th century knew how to work with water and there is still the sound of running water in and around the village. One of the tributaries of the River Calder (which means a fast flowing stream) passes through Spring Wood. The area is managed by Lancashire County Council with help from the Friends of Spring Wood. There are well-marked paths, glorious little private family places with picnic tables and information boards explaining the history of the wood and its wildlife.

Kiddiwalks in Lancashire

Getting there *From the A59 between Preston and Clitheroe turn off onto the A671 towards Clayton-le-Moors, Burnley and Nelson. Turn left at a set of traffic lights directly into the Spring Wood free car park. The village of Whalley is about half a mile away.*

Length of walk 1½ miles
Time 2 hours
Terrain Well-marked paths, suitable for pushchairs
Start/Parking At the Spring Wood car park where there are toilets (GR 742361).
Map OS Explorer 287, West Pennine Moors

Refreshments An ice cream van at the entrance to Spring Wood is usually, but not always, open. There are many places to eat in Whalley, however, with lots of old pubs, plus a good choice of cafés and teashops.

❶ From the car park, the route follows a well-made track that bears right and into the wood.

❷ Look to the right to see an outdoor classroom, guaranteed to provide interest and exercise for young brains and legs. The route now climbs gently through a splendid stretch of woodland. Sweep left through the trees and ignore the path leading to the summit of Spring Wood hill.

◆ Fun Things to See and Do ◆

Spring Wood is at its best in spring when the **bluebells** are in full bloom. In olden days glue was made out of the sticky sap of bluebells. It was used to fix the flight feather on to arrows. This was done by a man called a Fletcher. He passed these on to a man called a Bowman who made bows from the yew trees in the wood. The man who used the weapon was called an Archer. Look in the local telephone book when you get home and see how many of these names you can find.

In wet weather don't miss the '**Wellie Walk**' at Point 4. There is nothing children enjoy more than splashing about or playing hide-and-seek in the mud. Don't forget to take suitable clothes and a towel on days like this!

The Walk

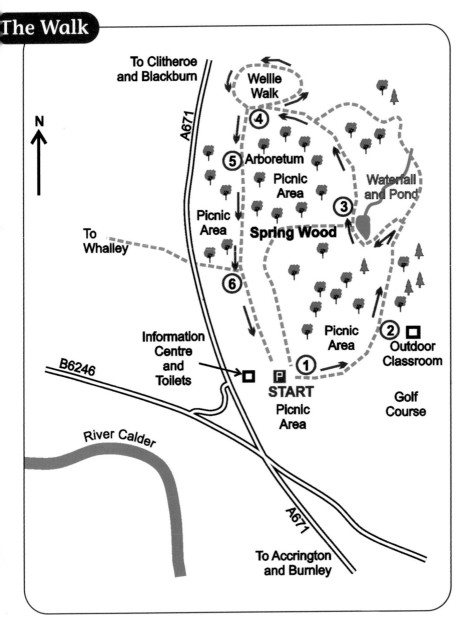

3 At the pond spend time at the seat listening to the little waterfall. Then bear sharp right. At this point the route starts to descend.

4 Here is a short diversion through the Wellie Walk. This is always a wet area and is a good place to look out for frogs and toads. There can also be plenty of butterflies taking nectar from the flowers that grow here in profusion. From the Wellie Walk take the obvious track down through the trees.

5 The Arboretum area is on the left. In this area of woodland are picnic tables and an information board to help with tree identification. Eventually the track descends out of the wood.

6 As the route levels out look to the right to see a gate. Above this is the A671 with a bridge passing beneath it. A very short optional diversion passes under the bridge to a pretty stream, which is an exciting play area for children. Return through yet another picnic area to the car park.

◆ Background Notes ◆

Background Notes

It is known that **Spring Wood** was in existence long before the 15th century and is part of Lancashire's original woodland. The then name of the wood was Oxheywood and it was part of an extensive deer park. From the 13th century the area was owned by the Cistercian monks of Whalley and there is a document pointing out that the wood was 'one bowshot to the east of the Abbey'.

Whalley can be reached from Spring Wood along delightful country footpaths. There is a Norman church and a mainly 14th-century abbey. The abbey was pulled down on the orders of Henry VIII in 1537 but plenty of the splendid structure remains. At that time much of the furniture was removed to the church. There is a wonderful set of carved choir stalls with misericords. In one, the carpenters show a monk trying to be a blacksmith but putting shoes on a goose! Another shows a man being hit on the head by his wife wielding a huge frying pan.

Foulridge

Not Foul but Beautiful

The towpath of the Leeds and Liverpool Canal.

B oats and birds, canal and cement, hide-and-seek and blood-curdling ghost stories combine to make this walk exciting for youngsters and gives them the opportunity to burn off some energy. Colourful canal barges can be seen at all times of the year and those in search of brave animals need look no further than Bluebell the cow.

Kiddiwalks in Lancashire

8

Getting there *At the end of the M65 motorway at Colne turn left and pass along North Valley Road with its shopping complex and fast food outlets. Turn left at traffic lights towards Skipton. Then take a left turn and descend to Foulridge Wharf on the right.*

Length of walk 1 mile
Time 1½ hours
Terrain Level and easy for pushchairs and wheelchairs to negotiate, though there is a steep push up by the village green.
Start/Parking At Foulridge Wharf car park (GR 887426).

The Walk

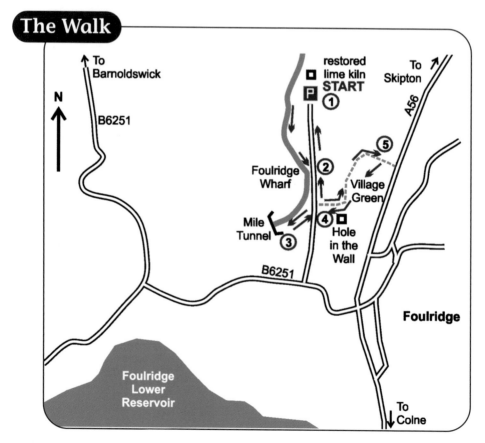

Map OS Explorer OL21, South Pennines

Refreshments There is a wide choice of places to eat for those who do not wish to take picnics. Three of the pubs close by are very family-friendly, including the Hole in the Wall at point 4 of the walk. There is also a good fish and chip shop and a snack bar on the A56 on the outskirts of the village. These can be reached by turning right from the steps at Point 5 on the walk.

1 From the car park head off to the right to reach the restored limekiln where it is possible to walk through the old workings. Eventually turn left along the canal towpath towards Foulridge.

2 Walk along the canal next to Foulridge Wharf. This is a fascinating place with old warehouses and machinery associated with the loading and unloading of goods. These days it is used for loading and unloading coach parties varying in age from pensioners to toddlers. They then enjoy a trip on the *Marton Emperor* which has a restaurant on board. It is possible to book a trip for parties (telephone 01282 869159) and there are regular trips that do not have to be booked in advance. The gentle journey towards the Skipton side of the Leeds and Liverpool Canal includes a journey through locks with a commentary on how the system works and the history of the canal.

3 From the *Marton Emperor's* berth look along the canal to see the entrance to the Mile Tunnel with its traffic light system. This is the time to think about leggers and of the swimming prowess of Bluebell the cow (see below). This is also the place to comment on the name of Foulridge, pronounced *Foalridge* – it was not

◆ Fun Things to See and Do ◆

Most canal barges have brightly-painted items of furniture on their deck. **Canal art** has long been famous and many of the boats are decorated in the 'Rose and Castle' style. It is great fun trying to draw your own canal art.

Kiddiwalks in Lancashire

a foul place! Long before the canal was built, the monks had a breeding stable here and it was then called Foal Ridge, a much more pleasant name.

From the Mile Tunnel return to the wharf and then turn right onto Waterhouse Lane and walk up to the Hole in the Wall pub.

4 At the Hole in the Wall turn sharp left on Town Gate to discover an old English village. Cottages are seen to the right and left of the village green. The houses were once occupied by handloom weavers but the place was also famous in the 18th century because of a group of very skilful tailors. Folk would travel miles from Skipton, Barnoldswick and the Colne area to order a set of made-to-measure clothes.

5 Straight ahead is a set of stone steps leading to the A56 and shops to the right. Do not go down the steps but follow the route as it sweeps right around the green. Continue to the Hole in the Wall. Turn right and return to the car park.

◆ Background Notes ◆

The walk passes close to the famous **Foulridge Mile Tunnel** which is actually 1,640 yards long and is therefore just short of a mile, but only by 120 yards. The tunnel was completed in 1796 and was the most expensive single structure along the whole length of the canal. It took five years to build and, with only their hands plus picks and shovels to work with, there were many accidents and a number of men were killed.

In 1912 a cow called Bluebell fell into the Barrowford end of the Mile Tunnel. She then swam all the way through the tunnel to Foulridge Wharf. She was revived with brandy by the landlord of the Hole in the Wall pub. A photograph of Bluebell, the brave cow who gave birth to a healthy calf only two weeks after her exploit, hangs in the lounge bar of the pub.

Wycoller

Folklore, Fact and Fiction

The packhorse bridge over Wycoller Beck.

This is the place where youngsters can pond dip, play Pooh sticks and hide-and-seek in the ruins of a famous old manor house, eat home-made ice cream, try to copy twig sculptures and explore the Panopticon built to represent the structure of an atom.

Kiddiwalks in Lancashire

Getting there *From Colne follow the A6068 towards Keighley. At Laneshaw Bridge find the Emmott Arms pub on the left. Turn right towards Haworth and cross over a bridge. Turn immediately right along Carrier's Row. Follow the brown signs to the free car park above Wycoller village.*

Length of walk 2 miles
Time 2½ hours
Terrain The well-made track into the village runs parallel to the road and apart from one short section at the approach to the village children can be allowed to wander at their own pace.
Start/Parking The car park above Wycoller village (GR 926395).

Map OS Explorer OL21, South Pennines
Refreshments The Wycoller Tea Rooms and Craft Centre welcomes children, those in walking boots, and dogs on leads. The comfortable café has been converted from an 18th-century weaver's cottage. Telephone: 01282 868395.

1 From the car park the track descends gently and there are seats on which to sit and enjoy the scenery. Just before the track meets the road into Wycoller look out for the flat vertical stones which still mark the boundaries of some fields. The road winds and crosses over a bridge.

◆ Fun Things to See and Do ◆

Wycoller Beck is a perfect place to enjoy a session of **pond dipping** or a game of Poohsticks. This is very safe and is close to the ancient ford which was in use long before the famous Wycoller bridges were built.

High above Wycoller is a global structure called the **Panopticon**, one of several built between 2003 and 2007 to provide viewpoints over the local countryside. This one, sited at a car park on the road between Haworth and Laneshaw Bridge, has a circular interior based on the theme of an atom. Children love to play inside and the views are spectacular.

2 To the left is a sign leading to Pepper Hill Barn and the base for the wardens. This is a place to explore the history of the area or to obtain any other assistance, including first aid. On the right is a small diversion along a tiny stream. This is where you may spot heron, kingfisher, grey wagtail and dipper, all of which depend upon the creatures which live in the river for their food. Pass many old and beautifully restored houses to right

and left before reaching the tea rooms on the left. Continue until Wycoller Beck is reached.

3 Look for the old ford and here there is a chance to do a little fishing with a net to find the invertebrates and fish that provide food for the birds. After this, cross over the packhorse bridge which dates at least to the 17th century and is one of the finest to be found in Lancashire.

The Walk

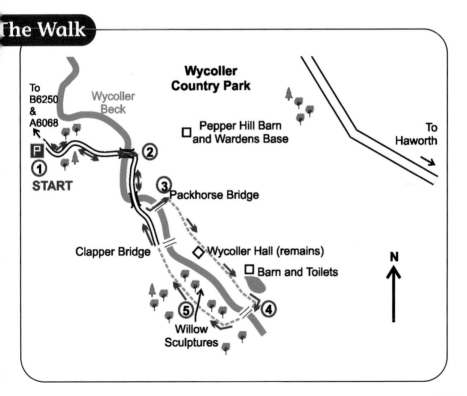

45

Kiddiwalks in Lancashire

Bear right and then left and pass right through the centre of the ruined hall. Look out for the huge inglenook fireplace, a feature of the dining room of the hall built in the 16th century.

From the hall the track winds its way around the 17th-century barn which is open to the public and is close to the toilets. Pass a pond on the left and bear right from the grassy track.

4 At a wall stile cross onto the old track that once led to Haworth and turn left. In a short distance turn right over a new but very pretty bridge. Turn right onto a newly created path. This has ponds to right and left and passes through an archway made out of tree branches.

5 To the right are sculptures of animals made out of willow branches. Follow the path and pass the clapper bridge on the right. This has grooves worn into the stone which are said to have been caused over hundreds of years by local people whose clogs have scraped away the stone. Bear left and then right. Pass through the hamlet and ascend the footpath back to the car park.

◆ Background Notes ◆

In the 1960s Wycoller was described as Lancashire's lost village but since the country park was established in the 1970s the old houses and cottages have been beautifully restored and the hamlet wins prizes as the best of its type in the county.

Why was Wycoller deserted in the first place? This was because those who lived there made their living from farming and weaving. This once kept the whole family busy. The men sheared the sheep and the children combed the woollen fibres. The women, called spinsters, then went to work on the spinning wheel. They produced the wool for the men to weave. Handloom weaving was a tough job and needed a lot of strength. The loom was made of wood and was a huge, heavy structure. Only men could use it and the loom was worth a lot of money. When a man died the loom was passed on to his eldest son. This is the meaning of the word heirloom.

10

Whitaker Park

Letting Off Steam

The East Lancaster Steam Railway.

ere is one of the best family strolls with good car parking, a museum and a variety of entertainments to suit all ages and physical ambitions. Youngsters will return home stimulated and tired – and all this for no cost! There is plenty of room to play games on the grass and the skateboard area is popular.

Getting there *Whitaker Park is about 500 yards west of the large roundabout in Rawtenstall on the north side of the A681 Haslingden road. It can also be reached by turning off the A56 and following the A681 towards Rawtenstall. There is a free car park.*

Length of walk 1¼ miles
Time 2 hours
Terrain There is a steep uphill stretch to the museum but the track is well made and fine for pushchairs and wheelchairs.
Start/Parking The car park at Whitaker Park (GR 226805).
Map OS Explorer OL21, South Pennines
Refreshments There is no café in the park itself but there is plenty of space for picnics. There are places to eat in Rawtenstall and cafés on the station of the East Lancashire Railway.

❶ Turn left from the car park and descend the well-made drive towards the A681. Before reaching the main road, turn sharp right and follow the track. There are seats beside the track, ideal for viewing the gardens.

❷ At the fountain look up to the right to see the museum that was once a house called Oak Hill set high on the slope. Ascend the path and bear right.

❸ The route leads past the front of the museum on the left. Inside there is a stuffed baby elephant, a reminder of earlier times when people were less worried about cruelty to animals.

❹ From the museum the route sweeps left and passes toilets on the left and a picnic area on the right. This is a wonderful area for small children because within sight of parents they can wander safely around enclosures containing rabbits and colourful small birds. Bear left and continue along a sharp incline.

❺ Here is a well-planned skateboard area. The track continues to ascend and reaches first a basketball court and then an adventure playground. The route then sweeps right, close to a football field on the left and a grassy area on the right. There is plenty of space for families who want to enjoy a picnic. The route then descends back to the car park and passes a well-kept bowling green on the left and tennis courts on the right which are free to those who bring their own equipment.

The Walk

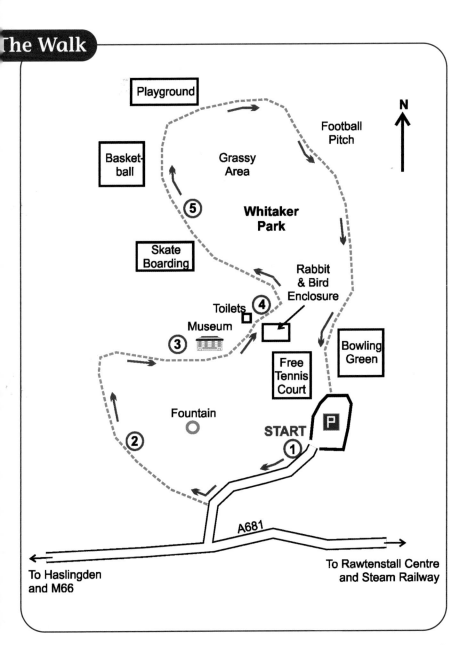

Playground

Basket-ball

Grassy Area

Football Pitch

N

Whitaker Park

⑤

Skate Boarding

Toilets

④

Museum

③

Rabbit & Bird Enclosure

Bowling Green

Free Tennis Court

Fountain

START

①

P

②

A681

To Haslingden and M66

To Rawtenstall Centre and Steam Railway

Rossendale Museum sits in tranquil parkland.

◆ Fun Things to See and Do ◆

In Rawtenstall there is an 18th-century loomshop telling the history of wool spinning and handloom weaving. It is called the **Weaver's Cottage** and was set up by the Rawtenstall Civic Society. There are demonstrations and lots of old pictures telling the history of Rossendale in days gone by.

Rawtenstall is the terminus of the **East Lancashire Railway**, a steam-operated line which runs on to Bury and Heywood via Ramsbottom (telephone 0161 764 7790). Refreshments are available at each station and on the train itself, although a picnic can be enjoyed on the move. Teddy Bears' picnics and Santa weekends have long been a feature. There is parking at all the larger stations en route.

Background Notes ◆

Whitaker Park contains the impressive **Rossendale Museum**. The museum was opened in 1902 in a house called Oak Hill that was once owned by prosperous mill owners. This relates to the time when the whole of Rossendale was covered by a canopy of trees dominated by splendid oaks. Indeed the name of nearby Accrington means a settlement surrounded by oaks – the fruit of the oak being 'acorns'.

Oak Hill was built in 1840 for George Hardman on a site overlooking his woollen mill at New Hall Hey. The word 'hey' means a woodland clearing. Later this area became dominated by cotton and when the Hardmans sold their estate it was bought by Richard Whitaker who later gave it to his home town to be used as a park and museum. The museum is open free of charge but is closed every Monday except Bank Holidays (telephone 01706 217777).

The original estate comprised 28 acres and included an area on the opposite side of the old road to Haslingden. This area is now occupied by Ski Rossendale, a dry ski slope which is very popular with youngsters.

Inside the Rossendale Museum are rooms furnished in the Victorian style and a collection of old toll boards showing what it cost to travel on the roads between 1780 and 1880. Young people will be fascinated by the collection of home-made musical instruments dating from the 18th century when commercially-made instruments were far too expensive for ordinary people. One is a woodwind instrument called a 'serpent'. It was wrapped around the player's neck and made them look as if they were being strangled by a huge snake!

Roddlesworth

A Hide-and-Seek Hamlet

Darwen Tower atop the hill.

This waymarked trail leads through fields, woodlands and along a pretty stream spanned by quaint bridges, one close to an ancient ford. Now set in quiet countryside, the area was once very busy. Youngsters can have lots of fun finding the ruined cottages at Halliwell Fold and the manor house of Hollinshead Hall. There is an extensive reservoir at Upper Roddlesworth with plenty of quiet little inlets and secret places to enjoy a game of hide-and-seek.

Roddlesworth

Getting there *About 5 miles south of Junction 3 of the M65, on the A675 towards Bolton, turn west on a road signed to Tockholes. It is also signed off the Blackburn to Darwen road (A666). There is plenty of free parking between the Royal Arms and the information centre which are about a mile south of Tockholes at Ryal Fold.*

Length of walk 2 miles
Time 3 hours
Terrain Very easy with just a few moderate ascents and descents.
Start/Parking At the car park (GR 665215).
Map OS Explorer 287, West Pennine Moors
Refreshments The information centre has an excellent café serving locally sourced child-friendly food. There are picnic tables all round the centre for those who want to eat in the open air or who have a dog with them. The car park is shared with the Royal Arms pub which also has a family-friendly menu.

1 In the car park look up to the east to see Darwen Tower on the hill. This looks like a space ship about to take off. It was built in 1897 to celebrate Queen Victoria's Diamond Jubilee. From the car park take care to cross the normally quiet but narrow road and pass through a kissing gate. The wide track bears left and descends through trees and areas full of flowers in the spring and summer.

2 At Halliwell Fold and bridge take time to search among the undergrowth to find the ruins of the old mill workers' houses. Also look out for old quarries that were important when the Lancashire towns were being built. Huge slabs were cut by hand to make street pavements. Some of these paving stones can be seen around the bridge and up to Hollinshead Hall. The cobbled road to the hall was also quarried locally. Climb the gentle slope with the river on the right. Continue for under half a mile.

3 Hollinshead Hall is a place to linger. Be sure to look at the well house. Retrace your steps to Halliwell Fold Bridge. Cross the bridge and turn right. Pass through extensive woodlands, full of wildlife even though most of the trees are conifers planted to prevent erosion undermining the foundations of the reservoir.

4 Approach a bridge over a stream. Cross the bridge and turn

The Walk

left. This ascends to the reservoir which is ideal for birdwatching.

5 The Roddlesworth reservoirs were constructed in the 1860s to provide essential water for the expanding Lancashire cotton towns and for the even faster growing city of Liverpool. The plantations, now the home of jays, woodpeckers and nuthatches, were planted around 1900 and consist of 200 acres with lots of clearings where spring flowers grow, especially bluebells. Although dominated by conifers, it is worth looking out for native trees including rowan, birch and oak. The stream leading out of the reservoir is the home of dippers and kingfishers whilst the reservoir itself is popular with anglers and birdwatchers. From the reservoir stroll along the obvious track through Tockholes Plantation and back to the starting point.

The Information Centre at the start of the walk.

◆ Fun Things to See and Do ◆

Between Halliwell Bridge and the ford is an area popular with local children who bring table tennis balls or use twigs to play **Pooh sticks** and hold competitions, timing the journey of each by counting the seconds. The water is shallow enough to be safe and children can play this game on their own.

The ruined Hollinshead Hall is a perfect place for a game of **hide-and-seek**. Look out for the old kitchen garden which has an orchard with fruit trees still in a healthy condition. Children love to picnic in the ruins of the house and compare what they are eating with the fruit grown in the orchards of the old hall that are still very much in evidence.

At Roddlesworth Upper reservoir there are plenty of quiet stretches away from wildlife where a game of **'skim the pebble'** can be enjoyed using the plentiful small flat stones.

During the walk youngsters get lots of fun seeking out the **oak trees** among the many conifers. This is also a pleasant stroll in winter when the conifers still have leaves whilst all that can be seen of the oaks is their bare branches.

◆ Background Notes ◆

The area is set close to the ancient Anglo-Saxon hamlet of **Tockholes**. This was one owned by a man called Touches and his home was in the hollow (or sheltered 'hole').

The lord of the local manor lived at **Hollinshead Hall** which is now ruined but is a wonderful place for children to explore what is left of the old house. There is a 'well house' which still has a spring trickling away inside it. The water pours out through the mouth of a beautifully carved lion. The water is said to possess healing qualities especially for those suffering from eye complaints. Pilgrims visited the spring long before the house was built. Their visits date back to Roman times nearly 2000 years ago, and perhaps even earlier.

Hollin is the old Anglo-Saxon word for holly and children can be asked to look for holly trees which still grow in the area. The present ruins are part of a hall built in the 18th century, which had extensive gardens and a huge orchard.

There is also a **ghost story** to curdle the blood. A horseman rode up to the hall on a wet and windy night only to find not one but six ghosts lined up to prevent him entering. He fled thinking that the spirits were angry that someone had built a house too near to their sacred well.

Fairhaven Lake

A Fairhaven Frolic

The RSPB Discovery Centre seen across the lake.

This easy circular walk offers seaside views and an amble around a lake created from an old flooded golf course. There is an adventure playground to use up energy and the opportunity for a game of crazy golf. There are wild places to explore and plenty of bird life to provide interest for one and all.

Getting there *From the M55 turn off at Junction 4 and head to South Shore and Lytham St Anne's. Follow the A5230 passing Pontin's Holiday Camp on the left. Continue until you see a large white church on the right. Follow the Fairhaven Lake signs. Cross the A584 and enter the pay and display Fairhaven Lake car park.*

The Walk

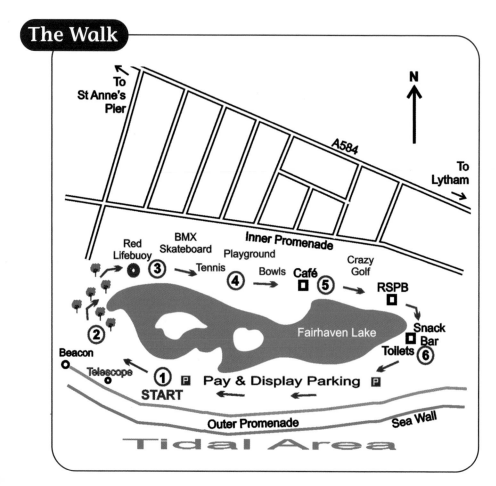

Fairhaven Lake

Length of walk 1¾ miles
Time 2½ hours
Terrain Level, with wide paths; suitable for pushchairs
Starting/Parking At the very end of the car park on the south side of the lake (GR 340273).
Map OS Explorer 286, Blackpool & Preston
Refreshments There is a snack bar at the entrance to the car park and a delightfully clean and family-friendly café.

1 From the west end of the car park take the first right turn and descend gently between trees to reach the lake. Just before the turn there is a coin-operated telescope from which there are splendid views across the Ribble estuary to Southport. Around the telescope there are large stones with seashells set into them.

2 See the beacon high up on the left and close to the promenade. The obvious path twists among trees with lots of secluded picnic tables. There are child-friendly areas among the trees ideal for dens and hide-and-seek. Young legs can be exercised in safety whilst older limbs can rest quietly on the seats and enjoy the wildlife.

3 The route swings to the right to reach a prominent red lifebuoy to the left. The lake is on the right and here is the launching point for the Blackpool and Fylde Model Boat Club. Even more at home on the water are birds such as the resident moorhen, coot, mallard and mute swans. They have plenty of safe nesting sites on the islands in the middle of the lake.

◆ Fun Things to See and Do ◆

At Fairhaven itself the **RSPB Discovery Centre** encourages the young to head out into the area to watch for wildlife. There is plenty to see when the tide is in, with the waves lapping against the sea wall. Some waves are more powerful than others and children may enjoy counting to see if it is true that every seventh wave is a big one. When the tide is out, fun can be had collecting colourful seashells. These can be pushed into modelling clay and painted to make attractive ornaments.

4 Continue along the obvious path to reach a white building on the left. Here is the base for a series of amenities to suit all tastes. There is a bowling green, tennis courts, adventure playground with lots of climbing frames and also skateboard and BMX ramps. There is yet another picnic site.

5 Keep the Fairhaven Lake café on the left and continue past the RSPB Discovery Centre which is open all year (except on Mondays). There is no entry fee.

There are leaflets and people on hand to help explain the history of Fairhaven and especially the birdlife around the area. The wide path sweeps to the right.

7 Approach the toilet block at the end of the lake. Ascend a few steps to the left to reach the snack bar. Turn right and return to the car park. Look out to the left over the sea wall to see the beach, the Ribble estuary and Southport on the opposite bank.

◆ Background Notes ◆

Lytham and the more modern **St Anne's** have been officially joined since 1923. Close to St Anne's Edwardian pier (1903) which has been restored, is a monument commemorating the wrecking of a German merchant ship called the *Mexico* which in December 1886 became stuck on the sandbanks between Southport and Lytham. Lifeboats were launched from both towns and all thirteen men of the Lytham crew were drowned and only two of the Southport crew survived. This was the worst disaster in the history of the lifeboat service and it directly stimulated the setting up of the Royal National Lifeboat Institution (RNLI).

The **Lytham Windmill**, with its cap in the shape of a boat, was built in 1805, the year of the Battle of Trafalgar. Its function was to grind oatmeal and wheat flour. In 1919 a gale revolved the sails so fast that the friction caused a fire which put an end to its working life. It has now been restored as a museum although its sails do not turn. Inside there is plenty to see, including an exhibition on breadmaking.

13

Mere Sands Wood

Look out for Merlin, the Magic Man

A bird hide at point 3 of the walk.

This is no 'mere wood' but was once part of a huge lake said to be the haunt of King Arthur. There are no Merlin magicians and no dragons these days but in the summer this is one of the best areas in Lancashire to see dragonflies. In winter, the bird life around the lakes is spectacular and the hides provided to view the birds are comfortable. The meandering paths through the woods have fascinating nooks and crannies and this stroll should keep active minds and bodies of all ages very busy.

13

Getting there *From the A59 between Preston and Liverpool reach the village of Rufford. At the very prominent Hesketh Arms turn west onto the B5246. Take care to drive slowly so as not to miss the left turn into Mere Sands Wood. There is an extensive car park which invites a voluntary parking fee and a ranger service on site.*

Length of walk 2 miles
Time 2½ hours
Terrain Very slightly undulating and suitable for wheelchairs and pushchairs.
Start/Parking The visitor centre car park (GR 447159).
Map OS Explorer 285, Southport & Chorley
Refreshments There are no refreshments at Mere Sands but there are places for those who bring their own picnic. There is the family-friendly Hesketh Arms pub in Rufford and cafés at the nearby Windmill Animal Farm and at the Martin Mere Wildfowl and Wetlands Reserve.

1 From the car park head towards the exit and then turn sharp right onto an obvious footpath which meanders through the woods, with fertile fields to the left.

2 Look to the right and see an observation platform. Take this very short cul-de-sac and enjoy views of the Mere End pond. There are birds to see all the year round, whilst in the warmer months there are dragonflies and damselflies. Return to the main path and turn right. The path is easy to follow and the trees on either side are places to watch grey squirrels. The path swings to the right.

3 Another short cul-de-sac diversion leads to a very large bird hide. Inside are benches and windows which open (please shut these before you leave). The walls are decorated with colourful pictures of the birds which can be seen around Mere End and visitors may be lucky enough to see kingfishers which are resident hereabouts. Return to the main path and look out for nesting boxes placed high in the trees. Follow the signs indicating Rufford village and follow the meandering path.

4 To the right are trees where youngsters can play hide-and-seek in safety whilst to the left are corn fields and views over to the village with its attractive houses and cricket field.

The Walk

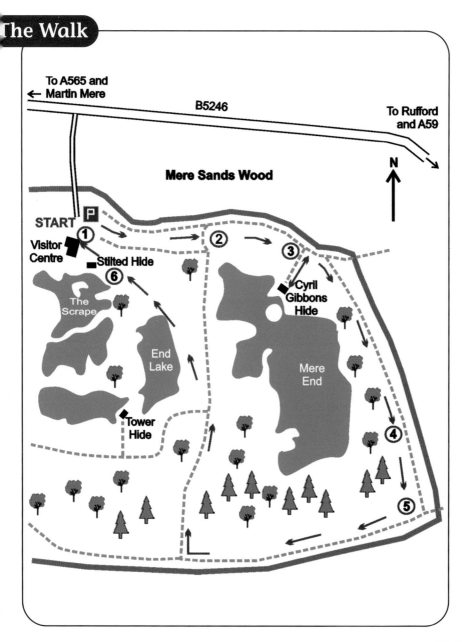

Kiddiwalks in Lancashire

◆ Fun Things to See and Do ◆

Inside the **visitor centre** are free leaflets dealing with the history of the site and showing the bats, wild flowers, moths and dragonflies which are common in the area. When taken home these can be used to produce a scrap book or a collage.

Keep a wary eye open for **red squirrels**. Red squirrels are becoming very much more rare as they have suffered from a virus disease that does not affect the grey squirrels. Reds are much smaller than the greys, but the best way to tell the difference is to look at the ears. Red squirrels have long hairy tufts on their ears and these are totally absent in the greys. Children's sharp eyes are much better at spotting the difference than those of adults.

Dragonflies and the smaller **damselflies** are very common here. There are red and blue damselflies and lots of fun can be had counting these. How many reds are there? How many blues? This game can be played around all of the stretches of water seen on the walk.

Very close by is the **Windmill Animal Farm** still dominated by the tower of the mill, which once ground flour. Here there is a display of farm animals and a huge adventure playground. There are tractor rides and animals, many of them friendly enough to be touched.

Just to the south of the Windmill Animal Farm is **Martin Mere** – the Wildfowl and Wetland Trust's reserve, famous for its collection of birds and for the huge flocks of pink footed geese and whooper swans that come from their breeding grounds in the Arctic, Scandinavia and Russia to winter at the reserve. There is a large café, bookshop and 360 acres of wild countryside to explore. There is also an adventure playground with exciting tunnels to crawl through.

Around **Mere Sand Wood** youngsters can think about the legend of King Arthur and his magic sword, Excalibur. Merlin performed magic here and some say that Martin Mere was the site of the legendary town of Camelot. Youngsters can have lots of active fun setting up mock battles.

◇◇◇◇◇◇◇◇◇◇◇◇◇◇◇◇◇◇◇◇◇◇

5 Be sure to ignore the signed route into the village and follow the path to the right. Also ignore the substantial wooden footbridge on the left over a small stream. This was once part of Martin Mere and is still a damp area. Cross several small wooden footbridges and then a more substantial structure. Ignore a sign which says 'short cut to Visitor Centre' to the right and continue straight ahead.

6 A large hide supported on substantial stilts overlooks the Scrape, another substantial area of water. Climb the steps and enjoy the views. Approach a signpost to the visitor centre, cross a footbridge and be sure to turn sharp left into the flower meadow where there are seats to rest awhile and look for the flowers and the numerous butterflies that feed on the nectar inside the blooms. Return to the visitor centre and car park.

Background Notes ◆

Martin Mere was once one of the largest freshwater lakes in England. It is said to have been the place where the dying King Arthur threw his sword Excalibur into the water. Who knows and who cares? It is just good fun speculating! It has been estimated that the shallow lake was more than 15 miles in circumference and there were lots of fishermen earning a living catching eels, roach, perch, pike and bream. These were sold in huge numbers from Anglo-Saxon times until the end of the 19th century.

All that remains of the lake today is the Wildfowl and Wetland Reserve at Martin Mere but the whole area is still wet below the surface.

As early as 1974 the Lancashire Trust for Nature Conservation decided to map the wildlife around Mere Sands. They worked closely with a company that wanted to extract high-quality sand suitable for making glass at nearby St Helens. The scheme worked to perfection and as the sand was extracted, the ponds, which are part of the walk, were created.

14

Astley Hall

On the Trail of Chorley and Cromwell

In the arounds of Astley Hall

his gentle stroll combines a walk through history, a stately home, gloriously spacious woodlands and a playground. What more could healthy young limbs need to enjoy themselves in so small an area? There are plenty of seats around for adults to sit and keep a watchful eye on the youngsters.

◇◆◇◆◇◆◇◆◇◆◇◆◇◆◇◆◇◆◇◆◇◆◇◆◇◆◇◆◇

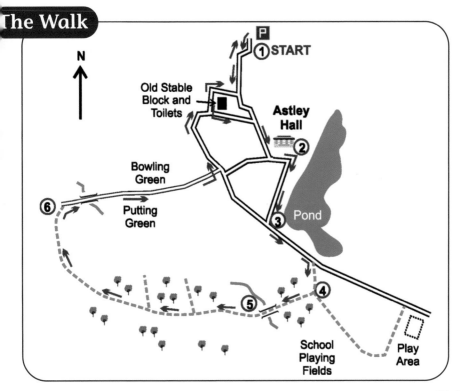

Getting there *From the M61 turn off at Junction 8 signed Chorley. Turn right at the next roundabout and aim for Euxton. Follow the brown signs and in about one mile turn left into Astley village.*

Length of walk 1½ miles
Time 2 hours
Terrain The going is easy except for one short set of wooden steps and there is an alternative path

there for those with pushchairs or wheelchairs.
Start/Parking In the large free car park close to Astley Hall (GR 575182).
Map OS Explorer 285, Southport & Chorley
Refreshments The old stables now houses a café and a gift shop. There are plenty of family-friendly pubs, cafés and restaurants in the town of Chorley.

The Walk

P
① START

Old Stable Block and Toilets

Astley Hall

②

Bowling Green

③ Pond

⑥

Putting Green

④

⑤

School Playing Fields

Play Area

N

Kiddiwalks in Lancashire

14

1 The first thing you see as you enter the park from the car park is the old stable block which is in an excellent state of repair following a lottery grant enabling refurbishment in 2008. The size of this building indicates that a great number of horses were kept in the days before cars. Pass an impressive cast-iron fountain on the right.

2 Astley Hall is seen to the left. Follow the path towards it and sweep right keeping the entrance on the left. There are few buildings as impressive as the front of Astley with its large number of windows constructed at a time when glass was very expensive. Ask the children to count how many windows they can see. Turn sharp right.

3 The ornamental pond is full of resident wildfowl and will be of special interest to young birdwatchers. Turn left and cross over a bridge surrounded by railings. Do not continue straight ahead but take the first right turn.

4 Look down to the right and follow a path descending to a set of wooden steps. After negotiating

◆ Fun Things to See and Do ◆

A path leads a short distance from the pond to the **adventure playground** where on many days an ice cream van is in close attendance.

Along the woodland section of the walk there is a fine display of native trees including oak, beech and hazel. Here is a good chance to learn to **identify trees** by the shape of their leaves in summer and by the colour and shape of their buds in winter.

Towards the end of the walk is a small **putting green** with equipment available for hire at the bowling club. There are seats all around the pond and woodlands which make ideal places to picnic.

On the trail near the pond.

the steps, you come to a modern wooden footbridge.

5 Cross the footbridge, stopping to take a careful look underneath where there is a much older stone bridge dating to at least the 17th century. This is still intact and was once an essential part of the route linking Astley with the nearby town of Chorley. Examine the bridge closely and you can see just how clever the builders of those days were. The stream beneath the bridge is a tributary of the River Chor from which the town takes its name. It simply means the meadow (lea) on the banks of the Chor.

From the bridge take the pathway to the right. Do not go up the wooden steps to the left which only lead to a school playing field. Continue ahead. This stretch of the walk is a delight as it strikes through the heart of a mature deciduous woodland, especially oak and beech. In the autumn there is a chance for youngsters to look for branches of beech blown off by the wind and note the long thin buds, which look like toothpicks. This is exactly what they were used for in the old days. Look out also for fallen beech seed cases. Squeeze one and you will see another reason why the folk of Astley Hall used the fruit of the beech. They contain a fatty substance which was used as an excellent furniture polish.

6 The woodland descends to meet a quiet narrow road (only used by vehicles visiting the hall and private traffic). Turn right and cross a bridge before ascending a steep track. On the left is a bowling green and to the right a putting green. Pass between these and see Astley Hall in front of you. Turn left and pass the stable block on the right before returning to the car park.

◆ Background Notes ◆

Astley Hall is one of the finest houses in the county and is open to the public. Footpaths wind their way through peaceful woodlands and by a circular pond. The extensive parkland is ideal for the study of flowers in the spring and summer and of fungi in the autumn. There is a variety of birds to be seen all through the year.

The building itself dates mainly from the 16th and 17th centuries. The entrance opens out into a spacious hall decorated with portraits of the period. Astley has a good collection of furniture including a 23 ft long shovelboard table. The game is played with a long stick, like a snooker cue, which is used to push heavy circular weights. This was a large-scale version of shove-halfpenny and the winner was the one who pushed the weight furthest along the table without making it drop off the end. Today's children could play it at home using a ruler and coins. Older children love this, whilst the younger ones enjoy seeing actors dressed up in Tudor costume which happens several times during the year.

Here, too, is a bed in which Oliver Cromwell is said to have slept when he was on his way to fight the king's men at Preston in 1648. There is also a pair of mucky boots on display which are thought to have belonged to him.

In 1922 the hall and grounds were given to the town on the condition that they served as a memorial to those killed in the First World War. Photographs of that war and a Book of Remembrance are to be found in a room at the hall.

Rivington

A Settlement by a Hill

The Old Barn Visitor Centre.

During this stroll youngsters can wander among the ruins of a castle and watch birds from the banks of a reservoir, as well as discover the history of a famous bar of soap. There is evidence of the Stone Age, Anglo-Saxon times and a story of a suffragette, the name given to those who supported the movement for votes for women more than a century ago.

Kiddiwalks in Lancashire

Getting there *From Junction 3 of the M65 follow the A675 to Belmont village. Here turn right along a minor road to Rivington. At the village turn left on Rivington Lane to reach the free car park at the Old Barn.*

Length of walk 2½ miles
Time 4 hours
Terrain This is suitable for wheelchairs but care needs to be taken to negotiate two slopes and short flights of steps. Otherwise the terrain is easy but undulating.
Start/Parking At the Old Barn car park. (GR 629138)
Map OS Explorer 287, West Pennine Moors
Refreshments The Old Barn visitor centre has a café and serves food every day. There are a number of picnic benches in the vicinity and an excellent outdoor area overlooking the car park and beyond it the reservoir. The café offers hot and healthy meals and excellent Kids' Choice options. There is also a café in Rivington village, with vegetarian options.

1 From the car park bear left and pass through the Go Ape complex. Sweep left and down a path to cross over a small stream.

2 Follow the obvious bridleway, ascend a gentle incline and reach the reservoir bank seen among the trees. Take time to watch for grey squirrels in the trees and wildfowl on the water.

3 Keep to the lower path which passes close to the reservoir. All around this lovely woodland walk there are seats, some of which have been donated by those who have loved the area. Look up to the hills on the left to see the Lord Leverhulme pigeon tower and the square tower which is Rivington Pike to the right of it.

Rivington castle ruins.

The Walk

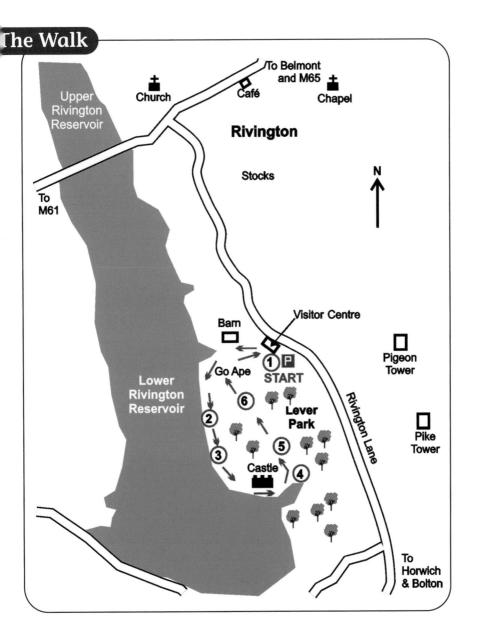

Upper Rivington Reservoir

Church

Café

To Belmont and M65

Chapel

Rivington

Stocks

N

To M61

Visitor Centre

Barn

Pigeon Tower

Go Ape

① P **START**

Lever Park

Lower Rivington Reservoir

⑥

②

⑤

Pike Tower

③

Castle

④

Rivington Lane

To Horwich & Bolton

4 The path winds its way around a replica of Liverpool Castle. Youngsters can play here for hours exploring the nooks, crannies, passages and archways whilst the more sedate adults can enjoy the views over the reservoir and surrounding woodlands. People are asked not to try and scramble up onto the battlements. From the castle the track leads straight ahead through woodland and eventually leads to another car park, but do not go so far.

5 You will see a footpath leading off to the left. Take this and continue through the woodland.

6 Look for seats beside the path. One of these is dedicated to the life of a lady called Edna Parker and from this seat take the second pathway to the right. Follow the upper footpath which winds gently with the reservoir on the left and returns to the Go Ape area and the car park.

◆ Fun Things to See and Do ◆

The **Visitor Centre** situated close to the barn has leaflets, books and displays showing the history of Rivington. There is a large model farm and youngsters are encouraged to play with this providing 'they leave it neat and tidy for the farmer'. The centre is closed on Mondays and Tuesdays except Bank Holidays.

In 2008 a new **Go Ape** adventure playground was set out among the trees. Whilst most of the complex is more suitable for those over ten, there is plenty for younger children to enjoy closer to the ground. There are staff on hand to help.

After playing prisoners in the **stocks** on Rivington Green, go to the churchyard and look hard for collections of stones. Nobody knows how old they are but some think they could be part of a stone circle dating back more than 5,000 years.

Background Notes

For the lovely walks we enjoy today we should give thanks to William Hesketh Lever who was born in Bolton in 1851. He followed in his father's grocery business before setting up his own Sunlight soap factories. These became part of the massive Unilever empire which sells its products all over the world. In 1889 Lever bought **Rivington Hall** and its estate. He kept 45 acres (18 hectares) for his own use but in 1902 gave the rest of the estate for the people of Bolton to enjoy.

Lord Leverhulme, as William Hesketh later became, was fanatical about preserving heritage and one of his pet hates was the fact that the expanding city of Liverpool had demolished its once powerful castle. Thomas looked out over Lower Rivington reservoir that had been completed in the 1870s and, in 1912, set about building a replica of the castle and designed it to resemble a stately ruin. It took 20 years to complete and it still stands on the banks of the reservoir.

There are two wonderful old barns to be explored. They are known to date to the 18th century but the beams have been dated to Anglo-Saxon times. Lord Leverhulme's idea was to have the barns renovated and used as refreshment rooms for visitors. This did not happen in his lifetime but one is now the café and bookshop. Great fun can be had looking at the beams and using one's imagination to think about what stories they could tell. During the Second World War both barns were used to store rations and soldiers from the Home Guard ensured that nobody broke in. Outside the barn is a very large car park that is used by motorcyclists, many with vintage machines.

Rivington is a delightful place with a village green and beside it the **parish church of Holy Trinity**, rebuilt in 1541 by the then lord of the manor re-using stone dating to the 13th century. From the village look up to the hills and see what is left of the Leverhulme estate, the gardens of which have been restored. Mr and Mrs Lever built a wonderful timber-framed bungalow but on 7 July 1913 a tragedy happened. The couple were dining with Lord Derby at his estate at Knowsley near Liverpool, when a suffragette called Edith Rigby set fire to the cottage and it was totally destroyed. It is said by some that the Beatles changed her name to Eleanor Rigby and made it famous in a song.

16

Hollingworth Lake

A Weaver's Seaside Walk

The firm path around the lake.

Water, water everywhere – and there is a real seaside feel to this family-friendly stroll. There are places to sit, a wide choice of picnic areas, woodland walks and adventure playgrounds. There are boat trips on offer and the chance to enjoy the sight of colourful yachts and canoes. The area is close to one of the finest stretches of a Roman road to be found anywhere in England. It is well worth devoting a whole day to Hollingworth as it is sure to fascinate children from 'nowt to ninety'.

Getting there *From Junction 21 of the M6 head towards Littleborough and follow the brown signs from Littleborough to Hollingworth Lake. On the B6225, at the junction close to the Wine Press Inn, turn east to Hollingworth and the pay and display car park in the village centre. There is also parking at the visitor centre.*

Length of walk 2½ miles
Time 3 hours
Terrain An easy circular track, ideal for pushchairs.
Start/Parking At the Watersports Centre (GR 934150).
Map OS Explorer OL21, South Pennines, or Explorer 277, Manchester & Salford
Refreshments There is an excellent fish and chip shop in Hollingworth and a variety of sandwich bars. There is a café at the visitor centre and others near the watersports car park.

1 Leave the car park and walk along the road through Hollingworth for about 100 yards. This is the only stretch of roadside pavement on the whole walk.

2 Approach the Beach Hotel on the left. Look out on the far right of the hotel for the obvious and well-made track leading to the lake on the left.

3 Follow the track and pass a number of seats to reach an area of the lake known as Queen's Bay.

4 Continue along the route to reach Shaw Moss Dam. This is one of the three huge embankments that have resisted the pressure of water in the lake since 1804.

5 Skirt round an area called the Promontory and look out for a building called TS Palatine run by the local sea cadets. The *Lady Alice* pleasure boat can also be boarded at this point. Cross Longden Brook by a footbridge and over the Rakewood Dam. Bear left, with the ancient settlement of Hollingworth Fold away to the right.

6 Turn right and cross the road to the Visitor and Information Centre with a café, bookshop, children's playground and toilets. Return to the road.

7 Cross over and see the attractive white-painted Wine Press Inn on the right. Follow the path and pass on the left the draw-off tower which drains water from the lake to top up the Rochdale Canal. Continue back to the start.

The Walk

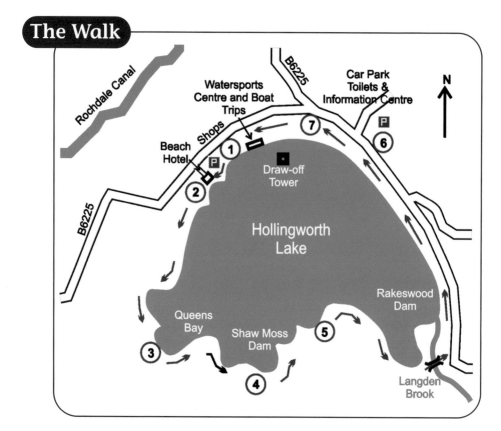

Rochdale Canal

Watersports Centre and Boat Trips

B6225

Car Park Toilets & Information Centre

N

Beach Hotel

Shops

① ②

Draw-off Tower

⑦

⑥

B6225

Hollingworth Lake

Rakeswood Dam

Queens Bay

Shaw Moss Dam

⑤

③

④

Langden Brook

◆ Fun Things to See and Do ◆

At the Watersports Centre enjoy watching colourful yachts and canoes. Take a **summertime trip** aboard the *Lady Alice* or hire a rowing boat.

At the visitor centre is a very large **adventure playground** and there are also bird-feeder days when families are given advice on when, where and how to feed birds.

Ducks aplenty.

Background Notes ◆

The **Rochdale Canal** was a brave enterprise completed in 1804. Its 33-mile length climbed up and down over the Pennines, requiring no fewer than 92 locks. Its importance was that it ran from Castlefield in Manchester to Sowerby Bridge in Yorkshire, thus linking the Mersey at the Lancashire end with the Calder and Hebble Navigation and the Humber at the Yorkshire end. The last commercial boat used the canal in 1937 but in recent years the Rochdale has been restored along its whole length.

The 92 locks required a vast volume of water to operate them and this is why Hollingworth Lake was built. It is 120 acres in size and can still provide two million gallons (around 9 million litres) of water per day. The water has proved a popular place to sail since Victorian times when it became known as 'the Weavers' Seaport' because of the cotton workers and their families who enjoyed their leisure time at the lake.

Jumbles Reservoir

A Rumble in the Jumbles

A tranquil stretch of water.

This combination of old Horrobin, hide-and-seek, horses, boats and birds, water and woodland produces an irresistible attraction for young and old alike. Footbridges can be crossed as footsteps echo from the span. There is the sound of birds in the trees and on the water and the trickle of streams running into the reservoir. There are perfect places to enjoy a good splash.

Jumbles Reservoir

Getting there *Jumbles Reservoir is at Waterfold, just north of Bromley Cross. It is reached from the A676 which links Bolton and Ramsbottom.*

Length of walk 2½ miles
Time 3 hours
Terrain A very easy undulating stroll, except for one uphill section between Points 3 and 4, but this is far from impossible although it is muddy following very wet weather.
Start/Parking The Information Centre near where there is a pay and display car park and toilet facilities. (GR 736140).
Map OS Explorer 287, West Pennine Moors
Refreshments The splendid little café at the Information Centre is open every day and has a surprisingly varied menu. There is plenty of room inside and lots of outdoor areas for use in fine weather.

1 From the Information Centre follow the obvious wide track which twists and turns its way between trees. This area looks as if it has been a forest for centuries but ask the children to wander around and take a closer look. Among the undergrowth are remains of old houses that were once part of the mill villages that were here before the reservoir. A good safe hide-and-seek area will certainly provide exercise for energetic little legs.

2 At the approach to a substantial footbridge look up to the right to find a little cul-de-sac leading to a bird hide. This is an ideal place to rest and play a game of 'Who can be silent for the longest time?' Cross the bridge and follow the winding and undulating track with more opportunities for strenuous hide-and-seek or, for the very young, a game of 'boo' among the trees.

3 Cross a very substantial footbridge over Bradshaw Brook and look out for a sign indicating that Turton Tower is only just over half a mile away. Ignore this but bear left towards a row of cottages. There is a steep ascent through trees but pushchairs can negotiate this except in the wettest of weather. Turn left and follow the track by the side of the reservoir.

4 Cross a small footbridge over a tiny fast-moving stream to reach the sailing club area. Here is a chance to count the boats and if sailing is taking place to identify the various colours of the sails and the hulls.

The Walk

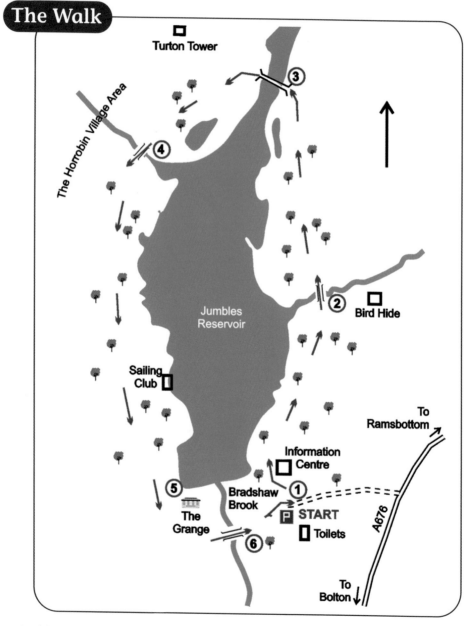

5 The Grange is the base for impressive stables. The people here and the horses know how to welcome well-behaved children. Continue past the Grange.

6 At another footbridge cross over Bradshaw Brook. The path first descends and then climbs steeply to return to the car park. If there are any children with energy left, a climb up and down the steps as fast as possible will ensure a well-earned rest in the car on the way home.

Turton Tower near the walk route.

◆ Fun Things to See and Do ◆

There are lots of **little streams** that move really quickly after rain. Here are the places to play Pooh sticks and have an energetic game of splash.

All around the walk are views of the reservoir and the chance to count both **birds and boats**, whilst towards the end of the walk horses will be in evidence.

There are several **footbridges** and lots of energy can be expended by first counting the number of strides needed to cross each bridge. Then a more energetic game can be enjoyed by finding how quickly the bridge can be crossed.

◆ Background Notes ◆

Jumbles Reservoir was opened in 1971. It swamped the large complex of mills at Horton and also a number of bleach works that had badly polluted the once beautiful Bradshaw Brook which was dammed in order to construct the reservoir. Jumbles now provides ten million gallons (42 million litres) of compensation water for the industries of Bolton. This supply is not used for drinking, thus enabling angling, boating and other water-based activities to be encouraged. A shallow area of food rich water had been set aside as a place for wildlife.

Gone is all the dirt and grime of industry and the once-derelict workers' houses are now much-sought-after cottages, set into a landscape that has maintained its olde worlde atmosphere. There are many footpaths plus a bridleway leading out from a riding centre on the banks of the reservoir. This is no jumble but a wonderfully peaceful place for the young to stretch their legs, whilst adults can watch them and envy them their energy.

Close to Jumbles is the impressive **Turton Tower**. This is a half-timbered Tudor house constructed around a 15th-century Pele tower built as a defence against the Scots at a time when England and Scotland were at war with each other. Turton was bought and restored in the 1840s by the Kay family, whose sons were great sportsmen. They had one of the best football teams in England and employed professionals to play for them. They also had tennis tournaments to rival Wimbledon that are commemorated in the Tower which is now a museum. There are collections of lethal weapons and suits of armour and, on occasions, early-Victorian life is remembered by school children who are allowed to dress up in the costume of the period and have a tour of the house.

Turton is not a jumble either, and neither the Tower nor the reservoir should be missed. The name Jumbles derives from a 19th-century corruption of **dumbles**. This means a fast-flowing stream cutting its way through woodland.

18

Haigh Hall

Wigan's Wonderful Walk

CAFETERIA

TOILETS

HAIGH HALL

CHILDRENS PLAY AREA

RAILWAY STATION

WALLED GARDEN

The entrance to the park.

This is a place of legends where two knights fought to the death. Added to this, Haigh Country Park offers putting, playgrounds, a railway and a ramble along wide, safe paths, surrounded by trees and open areas of grassland. Here is the chance to run around and then rest amid gardens and views of an historic house and to 'make Haigh (pronounced Hay) whilst the sun shines!'

Getting there *Leave the M6 at Junction 27 or the M61 at Junction 6. From Chorley and Standish use the A49 and look out for the impressive mileposts on this road. From the Boar's Head pub turn onto the road signed Haigh. Follow the brown signs and turn right along Red Rock Lane (the B5239) and cross the narrow bridge over the Leeds and Liverpool Canal. To the right is the Crawford Arms. Look out for Haigh Hall signed to the right. The narrow road leads to the large pay and display car park.*

The Walk

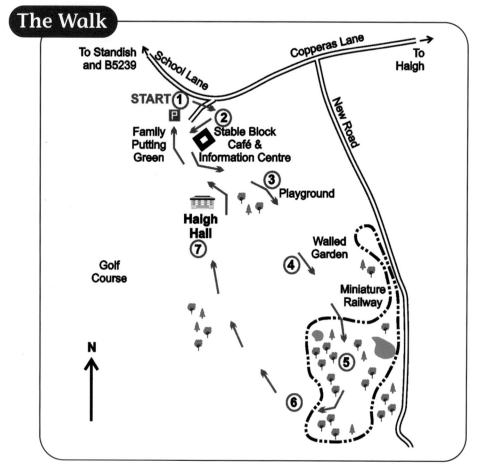

Haigh Hall

Length of walk 2 miles
Time 2½ hours
Terrain Very easy paths with no major inclines and plenty of places to stop and rest along the way.
Start/Parking The car park at Haigh Hall. (GR 595088).
Map OS Explorer 276, Bolton, Wigan and Warrington
Refreshments There is a good café in the stable block and lots of places to picnic in the area. The nearby Crawford Arms, set close to the canal towpath, also offers a family-friendly menu.

1 From the car park go to the park entrance which is on the left as you come in. Turn left through the gates and pass the golf professional's shop on the right. There is a family putting green on the right.

2 Pass the old stable block with its clock tower and turn left.

3 The impressive children's playground is on both sides of the track. Pass a pond on the left with water lilies and a fountain. Next on the left is the Crazy Golf course which is open during the warmer months and at weekends during off-peak periods.

4 Approach the large walled gardens on the left. Entry to these is through an arch. There is a picnic site to the right and, as elsewhere in the country park, dogs are welcome on leads. From the gardens the route continues straight ahead. The sign indicating the miniature railway should be ignored at this point. Cross the line.

◆ Fun Things to See and Do ◆

During the walk **collect feathers**. Whatever the species, there are two main types of feather. Look for small white ones that gradually feel warm as they pick up the heat from human hands. These are called down feathers and they keep the bird warm. The large feathers are called flight feathers or quill feathers. At one time they were used to write with. The feathers were sharpened with a penknife and were as important as ball point pens are to us today. Good fun can be had at home drawing pictures with watercolour paint using a feather as a pen.

A perfect place for a spot of fishing.

5 At the pond on the left there are plenty of birds to identify and it can be fun to listen out for the railway train. The path now meanders and then sweeps to the right.

6 Cross the railway line and see the station to the right. The route continues straight ahead and joins a wider track. Turn right along this and see the golf course to the left.

7 At the hall turn right and then left. Ascend the steep road and return to the stable block and the car park.

◆ Background Notes ◆

In 1188 the Haigh estate was owned by Hugh Le Norreys but it was Mabel, the daughter of his grandson, who brought fame to the family. In 1295 she married into the Anglo-Saxon family of de Bradshaigh. The Bradshaighs remained in residence until 1770 when the estate ran out of male heirs. It passed into the hands of ten-year-old Elizabeth Dalrymple and she eventually married the Earl of Crawford who set about mining a rich seam of coal. He also started his own iron foundry. In 1947 the estate was bought by Wigan Corporation.

Pennington Country Park and Flash

A Mine of Information

Just the ticket!.

Bridges, butterflies, boats and birds, reminders of the coal industry and the canal age, plus pleasant countryside make this a perfect stroll for young legs and eager brains. Add to this lots of playground space and picnic areas then you have the perfect slice of wild open space close to a very urban setting. The wounds of industry have been healed as a result of a partnership between nature and human planning.

Getting there *Pennington Flash is signed from the A580 and is only about a mile from the centre of Leigh. Turn onto the A572 and follow the signs to the Country Park. Drive slowly through the traffic calmers and over the bridge to the very large pay and display car park.*

Length of walk 1½ miles
Time 2 hours
Terrain Very easy except for the bridges up and over the canal where pushchairs have to be lifted but the steps are wide enough to ensure there is little difficulty.
Start/Parking The car park (GR 645991).
Map OS 276, Bolton, Wigan & Warrington
Refreshments At the car park there is almost always a snack bar serving hot and cold meals and an ice cream van sometimes. There are picnic sites aplenty including one close to the children's playground.

1 From the car park pass the information centre on the right but spend some time looking out from the seats overlooking the flooded flash which is now best described as a lake.

2 Approach the playground and picnic area which is situated on both sides of the path. Continue along the obvious track and approach the information board. Here the path diverges. Take the left fork but look out for the sculpture of the great spotted woodpecker fringed by trees. Continue along the winding track.

3 Approach the Horrocks hide with its entrance guarded by a wooden statue of an ugly man and enjoy a quiet period watching birds in an area called the Scrape. From the hide follow the tree-lined path, which was once the old railway track leading to the canal. Look out for a water level marker on the left of the path.

4 From the canal bridge look out over the water. This stretch was constructed to link the Leeds and Liverpool Canal and the Bridgewater Canal and ensure that coal could be delivered by barge to every cotton town in Lancashire, which was desperate for fuel as business expanded. Look out for the few remaining pieces of the Bickershaw colliery which operated until the early 1950s. Cross the bridge and turn right along the towpath.

The Walk

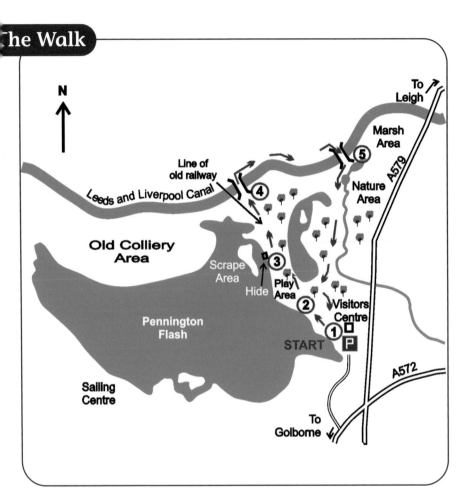

5 Continue until a second canal bridge is reached. Cross this and turn right. Pass through first a marshy area and then an even wetter space devoted to nature with lots of yellow flag irises which, together with the marsh marigolds, provide delightful splashes of colour in summer. This is a fascinating place to watch birds such as snipe and heron in the winter. Continue between belts of trees, keeping a look out for bird sculptures on the way, and return to the starting point.

Kiddiwalks in Lancashire

◆ Fun Things to See and Do ◆

There is an extensive children's **playground** close to the information centre and a chance to watch birds from one of the seven hides placed around the site.

Look for the very realistic bird **sculptures** including ducks and woodpeckers hidden among the vegetation.

◆ Background Notes ◆

Pennington Country Park was first opened in 1981 after much planning. The **Flash** consists of 170 acres of open water caused by the subsidence of what was one of the largest coal mines in Britain. The Flash is now surrounded by almost 1000 acres of varied habitat including a municipal golf course. The footpaths around have been landscaped on the colliery spoil heaps. These lead to bird hides and smaller ponds that are now used as breeding grounds for the coarse fish used to stock the main Flash. This has an angling club and a sailing club, and its bird life has been studied for many years by the Leigh Ornithologists Club. At the visitor centre the resident wardens have a blackboard on which they list the birds recorded each day.

At one time the whole of this area was devoted to farming with fresh water flowing from Hey Brook and smaller streams around it. Then coal was discovered and lots of muck and brass was the inevitable result. Subsidence was another bi-product of mining and so were the now grass-covered hillocks which are a feature of the Pennington Flash area today.

Mining for coal began in the Bickershaw area in 1820 and for many years railway lines ran around the site to make the colliery very profitable thanks to the export of thousands of tons of 'black gold'.

Moses Gate, Farnworth

A Paperchase at Moses Gate

Watching the swans.

Moses Gate Country Park is set in a very urban area close to a railway station and on a busy bus route but here you can enjoy walks around rivers, canals, woodlands and ponds. There are seats everywhere and a spacious car park. This really is a walk not just of promise, but of certainty, that youngsters will be active and happy.

20

Getting there *Leave the M61 motorway at Junction 3. Follow the A666 towards Bolton and through Kearsley and Farnworth. Moses Gate Country Park is signed from the road close to the still-operational railway station. Follow the winding track along Hall Lane to the car park.*

Length of walk 1½ miles
Time 2 hours
Terrain All the footpaths are signed and there are very few inclines so Moses Gate is suitable for pushchairs whatever the weather.
Start/Parking The free car park at Moses Gate Country Park (GR 743068).
Map OS Explorer 276, Bolton, Wigan & Warrington
Refreshments There are no suitable refreshment places in or around the park but don't let this put you off. Take a picnic to enjoy – there are benches and picnic tables all around – don't forget to add a little bit extra to share with the ever-hungry birds.

1 From the car park head towards Rock Hall Information Centre. The meander of the River Croal is to the left and time (and care) should be taken to explore the wildlife around the huge weir.

2 Reach the playground where even the most slow-moving of adults will get a burst of energy just by watching children making full use of the equipment. From the playground follow an obvious track.

3 Turn left and follow the gentle incline to the Rock Hall Information Centre. Turn right and then left and pass the Fishing Lodge on the right.

4 At the fishing lodge, stroll through the trees of the Adventure Nature Trail. Here there is a 'scratch and sniff' area where visitors are asked to scratch the surface of the plants and enjoy the smell. There is also a 'touch' area where the plants can be rough, smooth, hairy, have crinkly edges or feel sticky and there are also 'look and listen' areas where birds can be seen and heard. From the Fishing Lodge, bear right to reach the Wildlife Lodge on the left.

5 Enjoy the sight and the sound of birds such as mallard, mute swans, Canada geese, coots and moorhens. There is no shortage of picnic tables and the path swings right passing the Main Lodge back to the start.

The Walk

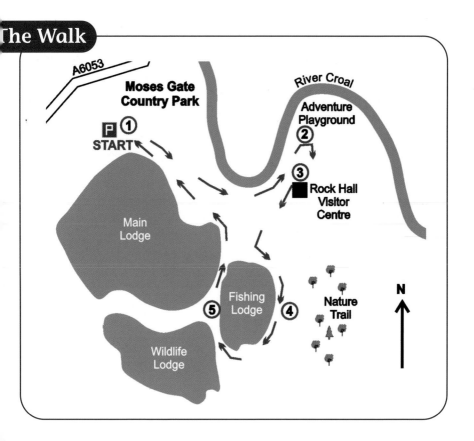

◆ Fun Things to See and Do ◆

There are free leaflets for children including a **Bingo Trail** where children tick off objects they see during a walk. These can be used as a competition or can be timed. The latter gets young legs moving at full speed! There is also a nature adventure trail. The Ranger Team can be contacted on 01204 334343.

The colourful playaround at Moses Gate.

◆ Background Notes ◆

At one time this area was packed with polluting industries including coalmines, cotton mills, bleachworks, chemical works and especially paper mills. These were all serviced by the Manchester, Bolton and Bury Canal which was completed in 1796. The most famous of these industries were the so-called **Farnworth paper mills** built by the Crompton family who also built Rock Hall, now the well appointed information centre.

At the information centre it is possible to trace the **history of the Croal-Irwell valley** back to the Ice Ages. As the Industrial Revolution gathered pace from 1800 onwards the Croal and the Irwell rivers, which merge near Rock Hall, became polluted but both are now clean. At one time there was a waterwheel, which has disappeared. Between Rock Hall and the adventure playground is the weir that increased the water flow for the wheel. This is the place to watch birds, especially the kingfisher.